395
1

D0442881

THE STRUGGLE FOR PEACE

THE STRUGGLE
FOR PEACE

LEONARD BEATON

FREDERICK A. PRAEGER, *Publishers*
New York • Washington

UNIVERSITY OF VICTORIA
LIBRARY
Victoria, B. C.

BOOKS THAT MATTER

Published in the United States of America in 1966
by Frederick A. Praeger, Inc., Publishers
111 Fourth Avenue, New York, N.Y. 10003

© George Allen & Unwin Ltd, 1966

All rights reserved

Library of Congress Catalog Card Number: 66-29734

Printed in the United States of America

CONTENTS

CHAPTER I

INTRODUCTION

A large part of the productive resources of mankind go into creating and equipping armed forces. Many millions of men are organized and trained as professional soldiers, sailors and airmen. Vast sums of money are taxed from the economies of the world to pay for fighting men and weapons. Machines of destruction have been perfected which could obliterate most or all of the human race.

These are the simple facts of our life. They have been deplored as waste and folly by thoughtful people for a long time. Governments have disputed means of disarmament over many years and occasionally have found partial measures which seemed to ease the pressure to match whatever rivals might be producing. But in general the levels of arms in the world have remained high, though this varies widely from area to area.

The object of this short book (and the television series it accompanies) is to state the facts of this situation. These facts are not simply a description of the forces that exist and the superb technology which the more advanced powers have been able to place in their hands. They are also the purposes for which this power exists; the ways in which it has been used; and the ways in which it might be used in the future. The fact that a weapon exists somewhere in Byelorussia or Kansas which can be fired at any point in the world causing immense destruction is perhaps interesting to the technicians : but the really important thing is why it has been built and what purposes its owners think it serves. So, too, with the Dutch Navy or the Argentine Army or the new armoured divisions of the Federal Republic of Germany. In many cases, of course, governments are quite uncertain about the purposes of their armed forces. They know merely that beneath the law and custom which dictates international practise there still remains a structure of power. Whether we like it or not, governments are the creatures of power. If they are overthrown by an internal revolt, they disappear : as in recent years the governments of Cuba, Nigeria, Ghana, and so on, have disappeared. If they are successfully invaded from the outside, as with Hungary, Tibet, Goa, and others, their whole position can be drastically altered. Such countries as Lithuania, Latvia and Estonia have disappeared altogether; and others, like Germany, Korea and Vietnam, have been divided by the facts of power. Men have long struggled to replace power by law based on such principles as the right of self-determination : but in fact they have succeeded only in so far as they have induced decisive powers to support these principles. If a structure of world law grows up and we achieve the peaceful settlement of disputes, it will be because those who possess power have decided to make it the servant of these things. They have already taken some major steps towards this objective.

The main purpose of this study, then, is to see what the system of power in the world now is and to ask what can be expected of it. If the answers to this cannot be clear cut, they are nevertheless important. They are about the prospect of survival and the nature of government if we do survive.

Let us begin with the broad facts of military life. They show a drastic contrast between the forces and expenditure in different countries. In most categories, the United States is the pre-eminent power. It spends $50b.[1] on defence annually followed by perhaps $40b. in the Soviet Union, about $5b. in Britain, France and Germany, perhaps $6b.

[1] This is the American billion: $50,000,000,000.

in China, $2b. in India, $1.5b. in Canada and Italy, $980m. in Indonesia, $700m. in Japan, and substantially less elsewhere. In numbers of men under arms and employed by the armed forces, the results are somewhat similar, though China and India come much higher in the list.

Four powers—the United States, the Soviet Union, Britain and France—possess nuclear weapons; and a fifth, China, is well advanced in their development. In most forms of nuclear power, the United States has maintained the supremacy she achieved when the first atomic bombs were built in 1945. She is also the prime naval power and has maintained enormous airpower. On land, however, there can be no doubt of the superiority of the Soviet Union in areas adjacent to the country itself. The most important of these is, of course, Europe. For the United States to reach the main disputed areas of the world, she must transport her forces across oceans, and she must supply them when they arrive. She is 4,000 miles from Germany and 10,000 miles from Vietnam. This means that a high proportion of her military effort must be diverted into the means of mobility—fleets, transport aircraft, mobile airpower. She cannot afford to lose the freedom to use the seas. In a long campaign of any kind, a high proportion of her resources must go into supply.

The effect of this organization of the American armed forces (and it also applies to Britain) is that she is a smaller power than the Soviet Union or China on their frontiers but can switch her power to other parts of the world relatively easily. Soviet and Chinese forces cannot be sent to distant places and still be effective against substantial opposition. The fact that the Soviet Union has never built an aircraft carrier is a reflection of a generally continental military organization. Though she has a large submarine fleet, it does not commit itself to the high seas for long periods of time. The long-range air transport fleet is very small. On the other hand, she has resources of firepower and armour which make her the predominant land power in Europe. As a result of the Second World War, she has pushed her front right across Europe to a line 100 miles beyond Berlin. She is still organized to fight a massive armoured and artillery war such as she fought in 1944 : but to this has been added large quantities of nuclear firepower directed primarily against Western Europe.

China appears to be planning to take the same road as the Soviet Union. Her level of industrial development must make it exceedingly difficult to evolve a wide range of modern military industries. She has, however, the basic industries needed to equip and maintain fighting soldiers. On the Asian mainland, she would no doubt have to give the command of the air to a sophisticated enemy (like the United States or the Soviet Union), but her massive land power would be difficult to defeat. Her limits were perhaps best shown in the contrast between the Korean War and the struggle for Taiwan (Formosa). In the first case, China competed on something like even terms with the United States and her allies. In the second, which involved crossing water, she was rendered impotent by the deployment of an American fleet in the China Sea.

In terms of size and wealth, four countries suggest themselves as a group : Britain, France, Germany and Japan. Although Japan's population is somewhat larger, they might all be said to have about 55m. people and a gross national product of about $70b. But they are in fact very different kinds of power.

Britain is far the most ambitious, having a substantial nuclear force, divisons in Germany, and forces and bases spread around the world. She is the only power which effectively shares the capacity of the United States armed forces to operate a long way from home. British forces have been involved in an almost continuous series of conflicts since the end of the Second World War. Some of these have been the general efforts of the Western world : in Greece, in the European confrontation (especially Berlin), and in Korea. But the main demands on British forces have been outside Europe : in Palestine in the post-war period, in Malaya during the long fight against Communist insurgency, in Kenya during the Mau Mau rebellion, and in Cyprus during the campaign for union with Greece. These were all responsibilities arising out of British rule. But there have also been many situations not involving British colonial responsibilities. British forces have intervened in large numbers in Malaysia during the post-independence confrontation with Indonesia; they have gone into Kenya, Tanganyika, Jordan and Kuwait at the request of the rulers; and they have played a major part in the United Nations peacekeeping force in Cyprus.

Since her withdrawal from Indochina and Algeria, France has been developing her armed forces along the same lines as Britain. She has been spending heavily on nuclear technology and constructing a modern rocket force to be armed with thermo-nuclear explosives in the 1970s. She has also been organizing her armed forces to have some capacity to intervene overseas. Emphasis has gone on aircraft carriers and light forces able to move over substantial distances. She has so far confined her overseas military interests, however, to the French Community in Africa.

West Germany makes a sharp contrast with both Britain and France. She has renounced the manufacture of nuclear weapons on her soil and has made no effort to develop forces which could be used outside Europe. Her armed forces have been designed for continental war on much the same lines as her main rival, the Soviet Union. During the last decade, the German Army has slowly grown in numbers to its present level of 300,000. This is substantially larger than the French and British armies.

Japan has much smaller armed forces than the other three. Where Germany has become involved in the confrontation between the North Atlantic powers and the Soviet Union, Japan has not been drawn into the American conflict with China. American forces are stationed in South Korea and actively engaged in South Vietnam; but they have not tried to bring in the Japanese with them. And though there has been some dispute over territory between Japan and the Soviet Union since 1945, this has not grown into a military confrontation. Japan, therefore, is non-nuclear like West Germany, she takes no part in a continental confrontation, and she has no capacity to operate far from home. Her armed forces remain at a low level. Many people believe that she is laying the foundations for the development of nuclear weapons. There is no sign yet of any desire to build forces to take part in the containment of China which is being pushed so anxiously by the United States.

After these countries, there is another group of industrial nations with well-equipped armed forces in smaller numbers. The leading examples of this are Canada and Italy. But Switzerland has very large reserve forces and so have Israel and Sweden. Belgium, Holland, Czechoslovakia and South Africa are well equipped small powers. Then there are very large armed forces in such relatively poor countries as India, Pakistan, Indonesia and Egypt. Latin America and Africa in comparison have small armed forces.

Arms industries have become an increasingly important part of power. Few countries can manufacture aeroplanes, for example, though small arms factories exist in most powers of any importance. A wide arms base is really only maintained now in the United States and the Soviet Union. Britain, which used to develop most modern weapons, decided to rely heavily on the production of her allies early in the 1960s; and of the other middle industrial powers only France has a substantial arms industry. Canada, Sweden, Italy and Switzerland manufacture a number of elements of modern power. But all of them are heavily dependent on outside sources of supply for many of their weapons. Outside the United States and Soviet Union, the drive for self-sufficiency in weapons production is most noticeable in the two very large nations : China and India.

The absence of highly efficient modern equipment is by

no means proof, however, that a country cannot use force effectively. With the possible exception of Korea, all the many conflicts of the post-1945 period have been primitive in character. Enormous sums of money have been spent on sophisticated weapons, but these have seldom been used. The pattern which has constantly been repeated has been one of first class armed forces finding themselves up against relatively simple enemies. Long and difficult conflicts have been waged by the French and Americans in Vietnam, by the French in Algeria, by the British in Malaya and Kenya, and by the Egyptians in the Yemen. In contrast with this pattern, India and Pakistan used their best equipment on the ground and in the air in the short Kashmir War of 1965.

It is believed by most governments that conflict is being held down to simple levels by the fear of nuclear war; but in most parts of the world this has not led governments to give up the vast expense of high-performance conventional weapons. The great powers still feel the need for three things all at once : substantial numbers of nuclear weapons; the main kinds of heavy conventional forces which were predominant in the Second World War; and light mobile forces for use in mountains and jungles.

All force exists now in the shadow—or under the umbrella—of nuclear weapons. Any study of the modern world must take account of this startling revolution in the life of man which was foreseen in 1940 and became a fact in 1945. It is these weapons which in their constantly increasing numbers appear to have created a system of stability among the major powers and their allies. At times, however, they have given rise to a fear of surprise attack of a kind which imagination could not conceive and computers could not predict. The fact that these weapons exist has influenced all plans for using other kinds of weapons; and the prospect of their spread to others has been recognized by many world leaders as the greatest unresolved problem of our day. Inevitably, therefore, we start with the nuclear arms race. But equally inevitably we pass to the other forms of power which really have been used and which constantly influence the shape of the world. That is the scheme of this book. It is hoped that it will gradually reveal some of the outlines of the partial and imperfect security system which is working in the world as it now is and which is still only dimly understood. It may also show some of the ways in which it might be perfected.

CHAPTER II

THE BOMB

In the successful development of an atomic explosive, the allied powers of the Second World War introduced a new and uncertain element into force in our world. There can be no doubt, however, about the size of the change in the destructive power of man; and no-one has questioned the awesome character of that power since atomic explosives were dropped on Hiroshima and Nagasaki and led with dramatic suddenness to the surrender of the Japanese Empire.

The possibility of a chain reaction which would loose the vast power of the atomic nucleus had been foreseen for many years. But it was in 1939, the year the second great European war of the twentieth century broke out, that scientists working in Berlin published the results of experiments which suggested that a chain reaction might really be within reach. At first, the implications of this work were not widely understood. In Germany itself, the correct conclusions were not drawn all through the Second World War. It was in Britain that the implications were seen most clearly—originally by two scientists, Dr Otto Frisch and Dr Rudolph Peierls, who had been driven from Germany and Austria by the Nazis. With a third, Sir Francis Simon (who was also a German), they saw the main steps which would be required to produce what they described as a super-bomb. They were given the full approval to go ahead by the British Government and this soon became a joint Anglo-Canadian programme.

At that time (1941), the United States was not at war, but the British and American Governments were co-operating closely. The American study of the same problem had led to conflicting interpretations; but it was finally agreed that the bomb could probably be made, that the Germans were probably making it, and that the United States should not be left behind. The Anglo-Canadian and American programmes were gradually fused until in 1943 they were effectively unified under joint control. The finance, however, was entirely provided by the United States. The first bomb to be produced was exploded in New Mexico on July 16, 1945, and the next two were used in action on August 6 and August 9. Since that time, no atomic weapon has been used for a military purpose.

There is no certain evidence about what the Soviets did in the field during the Second World War. They were certainly doing research in these technologies, but they are not known to have had a weapons programme. It is likely, therefore, that the allied development was the only one which began on any serious scale before 1945. Soon after the end of the war with Japan, however, the United States Government published all the main details of its work and the general lines which any successful nuclear weapons development programme would have to follow. The British and Canadians, of course, knew this from their participation in the joint programme.

Whatever they may have done before 1945, the Soviet Union then began an urgent effort to produce atomic weapons at the earliest possible date. They exploded their first test device in 1949, a date which was considerably earlier than had been thought possible by Western experts. Britain, which had begun her own programme in 1946, produced a device in 1952. The Canadian Government took a formal decision in 1946 to confine its atomic development work to peaceful applications.

The shock of the Soviet nuclear test provoked a period of considerable uncertainty and fear. This was greatly increased by the explosion in 1952 and 1953 of thermo-nuclear devices in which certain kinds of hydrogen were successfully fused in the temperatures produced by what was then the familiar atomic explosion. The first hydrogen bombs had a power which was about fifty times that of the bombs which had done such damage in the Japanese cities. It soon became obvious that much larger weapons even than this were possible. The late 1950s were the scene of this race and were dominated for some people by the fear that one side might achieve some kind of overwhelming capacity to destroy the other. Both, indeed, might acquire it.

The race, however, ended quite suddenly in about 1959 : and it ended for a very strange and unprecedented reason. The side which was clearly ahead and which would have no difficulty in asserting its supremacy suddenly announced that it considered any further progress to be futile. The United States Government said it had no use for larger and larger bombs. What it wanted was reliable weapons which weighed less and took up less space. American atomic development began to progress along this line—one of engineering perfection of the explosive power already achieved.

For some time, the Soviet Union appeared to be progressing along the old lines. It exploded a 57-megaton bomb—more than 2,500 times as powerful as the Hiroshima bomb—and the American authorities revealed that this could have been a 100-megaton bomb. This particular explosion had been deliberately kept down to 57 megatons because, as Mr Khrushchev later explained, the 100-megaton bomb would have been so powerful that 'it would have broken our windows'. The big bombs were used by the Soviets to sustain their prestige. 'Taking into account the fact that the Soviet Union built a hydrogen bomb earlier than the United States, and most important of all, that the US does not possess superpowered thermo-nuclear warheads in the range of several tens of millions of tons such as those possessed by the Soviet Union, we consider our nuclear superiority over the Western bloc to be indisputable.'[1]

The third nuclear power, Britain, exploded a thermo-nuclear device in 1957. After that, Britain and the United States returned to the wartime intimacy which had been broken by the American Atomic Energy Act of 1946. This in effect brought Britain's atomic weapons information up to the level of the United States and made possible a steady cutting back in the British nuclear weapons development effort.

As the development of ever larger explosives was abandoned by the United States and Soviet Union, several new ideas about future atomic weapons development were put forward. Perhaps the most important of these was the idea of a neutron bomb—a bomb which would have so little blast and heat that it would leave buildings undamaged. It would, however, emit large numbers of neutrons and would therefore kill human beings. Thus an enemy's property would be captured intact while he was destroyed. Although this type of weapon was advocated by a number of distinguished scientists, the point of it was never obvious to military men; and so far as is known it has been neither developed nor tested.

There has also been talk from time to time of radio-logical weapons but these, too, have probably been rejected. These are materials which are radioactive and which can be distributed in a particular place where they will give off a deadly gamma radiation for many years. As weapons they have a number of disadvantages : first, they cannot be made to increase their effect when they are landed against an enemy—they are like explosives which are ex-ploding all the time, even in the hands of those who are firing them; secondly, they run down steadily in power over the years and if they are not used must be put back into nuclear reactor to recover their strength; and thirdly,

[1] *Military Strategy*: ed. by Marshal V. D. Sokolovsky, Pall Mall Press, London, pp. 186–7.

they go on doing damage long after they are wanted. Nevertheless, it was feared that if the Germans had nuclear reactors they might have distributed radioactive Cobalt or some such agent on the Normandy beaches; General MacArthur suggested laying a broad strip of this material across Korea; and there has been talk of radiological materials being considered by the Egyptians for their rocket weapons against Israel.

The stabilization of the nuclear weapons development race among the three original nuclear powers was confirmed by their signature in 1963 of a ban on nuclear tests which most other countries have signed. However, two other powers had in the meantime formally embarked on nuclear weapons development and refused to adhere to this treaty. These were France and China. This and the mood of a number of other governments led the original nuclear powers to the conclusion in the 1960s that the main danger was not the weapons competition among themselves but the spread of nuclear weapons to a large number of countries.

The first French nuclear device was exploded in 1960. The thermo-nuclear test programme is planned to begin in 1967 in Polynesia, in the Pacific Ocean. The first Chinese nuclear test was successfully carried out in 1964 and a second soon after.

What other countries will follow in the footsteps of the first five and produce nuclear weapons? This obviously depends very much on who has the industrial capacity to sustain a major effort of this kind. There are many countries which would obviously like to have nuclear weapons but which have no way at present of acquiring the necessary material; and there are others with the undoubted capacity to make themselves nuclear powers who are not prepared to pay the price of building the weapons.

The two countries which in industrial terms could most easily make themselves nuclear powers are Canada and Germany. Both have large facilities and an advanced economy. Canada feels no need for these weapons, having on her border the vast committed armoury of the United States. The German Government has renounced their production, though it remains anxious to ensure that it has solid guarantees from its NATO allies. A third country, Sweden, has substantial nuclear capacity and an unwillingness to accept guarantees from others; but the long and open Swedish debate about nuclear weapons has come down for the present on the side of abstention.

This leaves three countries which can be regarded as serious possibilities : Japan, India and Israel. Japan has strong internal political resistance to anything to do with nuclear weapons. But she has a wide and growing industrial base and does not find herself in West Germany's position of vulnerability. As long as they are under pressure from so great a power as the Soviet Union, the Germans will be wholly reliant on their American guarantee. This gives the Americans a place in German planning which they do not necessarily have in Japan. At the same time, the pressures for a Japanese nuclear weapons programme are inevitably growing. They have been helped by the Chinese atomic programme—not because most Japanese see this as a threat but because it has to some extent removed the stigma from nuclear weapons in the eyes of the Japanese left.

India has had a much more active and open debate about developing nuclear weapons. Much political opinion strongly favoured a full abandonment of India's anti-nuclear doctrines. A large and able atomic energy industry has been built up in the country, greatly aided by Britain and Canada under the Commonwealth's Colombo Plan of development aid. This makes the job very much simpler than it would otherwise be. Nevertheless, it remains a large undertaking for a country with India's resources. There has been strong resistance by successive prime ministers to the effort and to the expenditure which would be involved. The grounds for these objections must decline over the years as India's self-sufficient capacity steadily increases.

Israel is a great unknown quantity. She has a nuclear reactor on her soil which could produce enough plutonium for about one atomic bomb a year; and she has a great capacity to work in secrecy. Of course, a good many more facilities are needed besides her present reactor. Nevertheless, the reactor is a major element of any atomic bomb programme and has been built with extensive French co-operation and without any agreement restricting what is to be done with its output. It is just conceivable that the Israelis might succeed in creating a small stock of atomic bombs. The main impediment would probably be fear of what consequences this might have in the Arab countries—and especially fear of an all-out Arab effort to destroy Israel before the bombs were ready.

What happens in other countries will depend to a large extent on what the major powers decide to do. If they build nuclear reactors all around the world to supply power for various purposes, the capacity to produce plutonium will inevitably spread at the same time. Comparatively few countries know how to build these reactors for themselves. Even more than India, most of the countries which might consider having these weapons do not have the necessary industrial base. If, however, they are sold or given reactors by others, the situation could change.

Because of their concern about this, the major powers have imposed controls on the sale of both reactors and the uranium which is needed to fuel them. Canada and France have exported reactors without these controls, but it is likely that this practice will end. Countries could, of course, accept inspection and then at a later date renounce it. But at present the major powers can see no solution to this problem.

There is also a major effort to see that the essential ingredient, uranium metal, is not easily available for weapons programmes. At present, outside the Communist bloc, there are only three producers with enough uranium to supply a substantial nuclear power : Canada, the United States and South Africa. To them will ultimately be added Sweden, but at a higher price. Many other countries have smaller quantities. The most important of them are France, Australia, India, Argentina, Portugal and Brazil.

It is probable that the belief of the early 1960s that perhaps twenty-five countries would have nuclear weapons very soon was a major error. Nevertheless, it is hard to see how growing industrial powers can indefinitely remain non-nuclear if they do not have some share in the direction of the world order. The club of the non-nuclear is growing at present rather faster than the club of the nuclear. It can probably now be thought to include Canada, Germany, Italy, Japan, Sweden and India and within a few years it will probably be possible to say that such countries as Belgium, Czechoslovakia, the Netherlands and Australia might have been nuclear powers if they had chosen.

Either this list or the list of the nuclear will steadily grow : for the number of countries capable of an industrial endeavour of this size is bound to grow steadily. The world advances, but the job of producing nuclear explosive remains about the same. The spread of industry for which all governments are working is also inevitably the spread of nuclear capacity.

CHAPTER III

NUCLEAR DELIVERY

When nuclear weapons were under development in the Second World War, little thought was given to the problem of getting them to their targets. There existed at the time substantial bomber forces able to carry heavy loads either to Germany or to Japan. A heavy bomb of this kind could be carried either in the American B-29 (the aircraft used for the two atomic bombs dropped on Japan) or the British Lancaster.

After 1945, however, it rapidly became obvious that the problem of delivery would be very much more demanding. If the West's potential enemy was to be the Soviet Union, bombers would have to travel over much longer distances. Their chances of being shot down would be increased. The United States would have to rely on overseas bases. The Soviet Union, for its part, would have no chance of attack on the United States itself until it had taken its aircraft industry much farther.

This business of getting to the target created serious difficulties of both range and penetration. But gradually there dawned on the military planners of all countries a problem of entirely new proportions : this was the damage which the nuclear forces of the other side might be able to do to your own nuclear forces before they got off the ground. Both sides were resigning themselves to the idea that their cities could be destroyed; but it was argued that even an enemy able to do this would not do it if he knew that his cities would be destroyed in return. The logic of this notion of mutual deterrence was acceptable to most military thinkers and politicians. But if an enemy was able to destroy cities in a surprise attack, would he not also be able to destroy bomber bases? And in that event could there be any assurance of retaliation? And if there is to be no retaliation, where is the deterrent to the attack?

With the development of the vast destructive power of thermo-nuclear weapons after 1953, this argument became particularly uncomfortable. What was needed was a nuclear force which could (1) reach its targets; (2) evade interception; (3) do both these after being struck by the heaviest and most damaging blow an enemy could conceive. The attempt to meet these conditions constitutes perhaps the most advanced and ambitious technological development effort in history.

The United States, having the first bombs, made the first major development effort. It took its wartime bomber types to their limits and built hundreds of the huge B-36 bomber. In what later became the tradition of nuclear delivery systems, this was soon scrapped for a jet bomber, the B-47, which would be better able to penetrate the jet fighter defences which the Soviets were developing at high priority. (It was later calculated that in the nuclear arms race of the 1950s the Soviets spent about three times as much on defence as they did on striking power and the Americans spent about three times as much on striking power as they did on defence.)

After the Second World War, the United States had begun the development of a rocket weapon which might carry a nuclear weapon 5,000 miles—a vast and almost incredible extension of the German V-2 rocket which had been used in large numbers against London, Antwerp and other cities. This project was, however, dropped because it was argued that the inaccuracy would always be too great to make the weapon militarily worthwhile. This was an error which the United States came to regret bitterly. Where the American planners had miscalculated had been in rejecting the possibility of increasing the explosive power to be carried by the rocket by using it as a vehicle for the hydrogen bomb. If the rocket could have a thermo-nuclear warhead, it could obviously afford to miss by a larger distance. It was wrongly argued that the thermo-nuclear warheads then being considered could not possibly be reduced to the necessary size and weight for the rockets which then seemed possible. The error was realized in 1953; and the massive American rocket effort largely derives from that date.

The main advantage of rockets, or ballistic missiles, was that they faced no defensive weapons. They therefore completely solved the growing problem of penetrating air defences. But there remained the problem of vulnerability. The Americans began to grapple seriously with this in about 1956 : and it came to have a decisive effect on their strategic nuclear forces. They also decided to escape from dependence on foreign bases by developing a very long-range jet bomber and by building aircraft specially for the job of refuelling the medium bombers, the B-47s, in the air. The build-up of these bomber fleets went on at high priority with all the immense resources of American mass production. Altogether 1,300 B-47s were produced and 600 of the intercontinental B-52s. Gradually, the B-47 was freed from dependence on its bases which were mainly in England but also in Spain, Morocco, Saudi Arabia and Guam. The whole force was permanently based in the United States after about 1959.

Thinking in traditional air force terms, the USAF looked forward to bombers which could fly higher and faster to replace the B-47 and B-52. They designed and began to develop a supersonic medium bomber, the B-58 Hustler, to replace the B-47, and a supersonic heavy bomber, the B-70 Valkyrie, to replace the B-52s. But these were vulnerable on the ground to a surprise attack; and this problem would not be solved by making them fly higher and faster. The American Defense Department therefore became very sceptical about the value of a new generation of bombers : and a contributing factor was the heavy cost of keeping bomber crews in training in peacetime. Major Congressional battles ensued—first over building additional B-52s and then over the B-58 and finally the B-70. In the end, the numbers of B-52s were restricted to 600 and the B-58s to seventy. The B-70 was never built as an operational bomber at all.

The story of the missiles is equally stormy. When the intercontinental rocket programme, called the Atlas, was re-started in 1953, it was fortunate in being able to draw on the experience of an unsuccessful programme for a rocket-powered bomber, the Navaho. But it was still far behind the Soviet Union. In 1957, it was considered that a shorter range ballistic missile could be produced very quickly by using one of the Atlas motors and this became the Thor, the first major rocket weapon in the West. Sixty of these were based in England along an eastern strip from Norfolk to Yorkshire. Each group of three was put at least fourteen miles from every other so that no Soviet surprise attack could take out more than one base of three missiles with each weapon. These missiles were scrapped after about five years' RAF service.

By 1959, the United States had developed two other ballistic missiles in the same category as Atlas and Thor : the Titan and Jupiter. It thus had four missiles, two of which could be based at home and two in Europe. But they were all immensely vulnerable to attack; and while the bomber fleets practised the technique of getting into the air on the slightest radar warning the missiles could not be fired unless the ultimate decision to wage massive nuclear war had been taken.

It was then that a dramatic change took place which appeared to solve the problem of vulnerability. Up to this time, rocket engines had been using fuels which were so difficult to maintain that they had to be manufactured on the site. All four of these big American rockets had been of this liquid fuelled type and involved complex and expensive facilities. But by about 1959, the Americans felt they had solved the problem of building rocket engines which were in effect like gunpowder—stable in their cases over long periods and then powerful and reliable when lighted. This led to the simple, cheap and reliable ballistic missile which could be handled even in so narrow a space as a submarine.

In 1958, the decision was taken to hold back the large-scale production of Atlas, Titan, Thor and Jupiter while three of these new solid fuel weapons were explored. Each of these was a solid fuel rocket and each tried to find safety from surprise attack in a different way. The first, Minuteman, was to be land based: but it would be mobile in special trains so that its precise position would never be known to an enemy. The second, Polaris, was to be put to sea in submarines and cruisers. The third, Skybolt, would be based, in effect, in the sky under the wings of B-52 bombers. This extraordinary variety of solutions to the problem of vulnerability was bequeathed to the new Kennedy Administration by the Eisenhower Administration which went out of power at the beginning of 1961.

The best solutions rapidly emerged. First, it was decided that the train-mounted Minuteman was not worth the expense and that the more reliable and permanent solution was to bury them deep in special silos which could only be destroyed by a direct hit. Then the cruiser-mounted Polaris was thought to be too vulnerable, since surface ships can easily be constantly tracked. Finally, after much debate, it was decided that Skybolt only made sense if the aircraft were kept constantly in the air: and the expense of this was going to be very great indeed over the years. So the choice fell on the submarine-based Polaris and the land-based Minuteman. The submarines offered what seemed to be almost complete invulnerability: the Minuteman gave large numbers very cheaply. Minuteman would remain invulnerable as long as the Soviets did not build up huge numbers of weapons targeted directly on to them. Such a Soviet programme was possible : but it would cost them many times the cost of the Minuteman and there was no sign that they had any intention of doing it.

By 1962, therefore, the direction of the American effort had at last been settled. The big bombers, the liquid fuelled missiles, the train-mounted missiles and the surface ship missiles had all been dropped. It was decided that the heavy nuclear forces would be 41 submarines, containing a total of 656 missiles, and 1,000 Minuteman each in its own separated underground base. To this was added a deep command centre in the Cheyenne Mountains, built at enormous cost, and a permanently airborne emergency command post in case an enemy surprise attack utterly destroyed the entire political structure of the country and the command post as well.

Less is known about the way in which Soviet thinking has developed over the years. But it is clear that they have concentrated on what they conceived to be an essentially defensive task against the aggressive nuclear forces of their capitalist enemies. Their first nuclear bomber was the medium range Tu-16 Badger which was built up in large numbers for use against targets in Western Europe. Presumably, the most important of these targets was the Strategic Air Command overseas bases. The Soviets developed a true intercontinental bomber in the vast Tu-95 Bear and also in the jet-powered Bison. But to the great surprise of the Americans they seem to have kept their production of these down to about 200 while building up about 1,500 of the medium range bombers. This showed clearly that the main Soviet priority remained Europe.

Soviet rocket development was maintained on a continous basis from the German V-2 and developed steadily larger units through the 1950s. The scale that had been achieved became clear to the West through the space firings of 1957 and after : and it was these that provoked the fear that there might be a significant Soviet lead in rockets by 1962. The Eisenhower Administration was strongly attacked on this issue by Senator John Kennedy and others; but the conviction that there was no prospect of a deterrent gap even if there was a missile gap was speedily shared by the Democrats when they achieved power in 1961.

As it has turned out, the emphasis in Soviet liquid-fuelled rockets seems to have been about the same as it was in their bomber programme. They have deployed about 700 missiles with a range adequate to cover Western Europe : and these have been made mobile in trucks to give them some measure of invulnerability. There are many fewer long-range missiles able to strike at the United States— perhaps about 275. It is clear from these numbers that so far there has been no effort to build up a force capable of a successful surprise attack on the 1,000 Minuteman. This would take at least 2,000 missiles and even then it would have to be calculated that a small number would remain.

Almost the whole force of Soviet bombers and missiles appears to be vulnerable to a surprise attack from the West. With their belief that the West is fundamentally aggressive, this situation is unlikely to satisfy them; and it is generally assumed that they are engaged on the same pursuit of invulnerable weapons as the Western powers. Soviet submarines have been used for rockets but so far on a much smaller scale than in the United States. There appear to be about thirty in commission, each armed with three missiles. But it is generally thought that Soviet solid fuel rocket development must now be progressing rapidly and that weapons which are much less vulnerable will soon emerge.

It is seldom forgotten, however, that the Soviets have explored very large yield weapons. Western opinion has never been entirely clear about the purpose behind this. It might well be a simple desire to push atomic weapons development as far as possible. One other possibility has, however, been discussed. This is that the Soviets might want to put weapons into orbit of such vast power that they could destroy huge areas below them as they travelled in their orbit. The idea of putting atomic weapons into orbit and then bringing them down on to a target is one which has caused considerable public concern : but it has never appealed to the experts. It has practically every disadvantage. First, it is expensive to put them up; secondly, it is harder to get them down on to a target than to fire a missile from another point on the earth; thirdly, they are public and obvious and can be destroyed or even examined and defused by an enemy as they orbit in times of peace; fourthly, they can only be fired from a particular point in their orbit and so are unusable at a precise moment; fifthly, they would be exceedingly expensive to maintain in first-class working order, if this was possible at all. But a weapon which could be exploded in orbit would be much cheaper and easier. It would not require an expensive recovery system and it would give absolutely no warning. The Chief Scientific Adviser to the British Ministry of Defence, Sir Solly Zuckerman, has made public reference to this : 'Following on this explosion [the Soviet 57-megaton bomb] some experienced nuclear physicists let it be known that weapons with a yield of 100 megatons or more could be exploded outside the atmosphere over a country and, for reasons into which I need not enter, destroy hundreds of square miles of that country utterly by means of a single heat flash.'[1] Although there would be great disadvantages in it, the Soviets may have considered such a weapon.

Assuming that the Soviet Union is moving towards the United States in relying on invulnerable missiles, it would seem that the two have reached a balance. But there is one area of rapid technical development which could upset this balance. This is an effective means of defence against ballistic missiles. It is probable that the Soviets, with their anxiety for the best possible defences, are well ahead in this

[1] Lees-Knowles Lectures, 1965, reprinted in *The Sunday Times*, London, February 13, 1966.

technology. Strong statements have been made about the ability of the Soviet armed forces to destroy enemy rockets. The chances are that they can do this on test ranges but are still a long way from mass production of the necessary weapons for a defence of Soviet cities.

They are also probably unable to avoid being saturated by large numbers of weapons, especially where various forms of decoy are used. This, at any rate, is the situation in the United States, where the Government has resisted proposals that they should put their anti-ballistic missile system into mass production. It is being strongly argued in Washington, however, that while the Soviets might be able to overwhelm an American defensive system of this kind, smaller nuclear powers—which for the present means China—could not.

The third nuclear power, Britain, has followed much the same lines as the United States. When the British atomic bomb programme was begun in 1946 it was soon followed by a plan for a medium jet bomber. In fact, two of these were built, the Vulcan and the Victor, in case one should not be successful. A less ambitious aircraft, the Valiant, was later begun so that a British bomber force could be put into service in 1955. This V-bomber force was built up to about 180 and re-equipped with thermo-nuclear weapons between 1960 and 1962.

Taking the lead from the Atlas programme, Britain embarked on a large liquid-fuelled rocket, called Blue Streak, in 1955. This used the main booster rocket from the Atlas which was developed and constructed to British specifications. In 1960, however, it was decided that the programme was becoming expensive and the rocket (even in the planned underground bases) would be vulnerable. The Americans offered to sell Britain Skybolt. It was decided to acquire this for the Mark 2 Vulcan bombers and the Blue Streak programme was cancelled. When Skybolt itself was cancelled in 1962, the United States Government agreed to make Polaris missiles available in its place : and

c

the British Government decided to build five (later changed to four) nuclear submarines each to carry sixteen of these missiles. The warheads and submarines would be built in Britain, but the missiles themselves would be bought direct from their American producers.

France began her nuclear delivery system much later than the United States, the Soviet Union and Britain. She began a close study of the delivery problem in about 1958 and decided that she would build a supersonic light bomber for use with refuelling tankers to take her through the 1960s. After that she would rely on solid fuel rockets. The light bomber, the Mirage IV, went into service with the first French atomic bombs in 1964. A total of fifty of these are being built. The rocket programme is designed to produce a weapon which can be used both from underground bases on land and from submarines. The United States offered France the Polaris missile in 1962 on the same terms as her offer to Britain, but this was declined.

China has come into the field still later and lacks an aircraft industry which could easily construct a bomber. It is generally assumed that all Chinese development work for nuclear delivery is going into ballistic missiles and that these will come forward into service in the course of the 1970s. The United States Government believes that the Chinese will be able to strike at the United States by about 1980. If the Chinese have the range to strike at the United States, they will also be able to strike at any part of the Soviet Union or at Western Europe.

In summary, then, the present strategic nuclear forces are approximately as follows :

	U.S.	S.U.	Britain	France
Heavy bombers	600	200	—	—
Medium bombers	70	1000	80	—
Light bombers	—	—	—	50
Long-range rockets	1000	275	—	—
Medium-range rockets	—	700	—	Building
Sea-based rockets	656	140	Buying 64	Building

CHAPTER IV

CENTRAL WAR FORCES

In spite of the nuclear weapons on both sides, the largest conventional arms build-up in the world has gone on in Europe for many years. Immense sums of money have been spent equipping forces up to the best modern standards. The armies of both the North Atlantic Treaty powers and the Warsaw Pact powers have been given enough vehicles to enable them to move at high speed across the ground. Very large air forces have been constructed with high performance aircraft both for strike and for interception. Long and expensive supply lines have been laid down and equipped for a major struggle. In the case of the NATO powers, this has meant achieving both the ability to dominate the Atlantic ocean and the capacity to transport large loads by air and sea. Modern armies depend on huge quantities of fuel; and pipelines have been built to supply the airfields with large quantities of fuel.

In numbers of men and divisions, this confrontation in Germany and the countries on each side of it is approximately as follows :

		divisions	men
Warsaw Pact	Soviet Union	26	600,000
	East Germany	6	80,000
	Poland	14	220,000
	Czechoslovakia	14	200,000
	Hungary	6	100,000
	TOTAL	66	1,200,000

		divisions	*men*
NATO:	West Germany	12	275,000
	United States	6	240,000
	France	5	250,000
	Britain	3	55,000
	Holland	2	90,000
	Belgium	2	80,000
	Canada	½	10,000
		33½	1,000,000

There has been much argument about who has the predominance or who ought to have it. This cannot be assessed from numbers of men. Equipment is exceedingly important : and so are such things as the state of training, which will depend with conscript armies on the time the troops have been in service. Any trial of arms would also depend on who was expecting it and who struck first. Nevertheless, there has never been any real reason to doubt that the main military force in Europe is the Soviet Army, which has 2,000,000 men and two years service (which means that a higher proportion are trained than is the case with the 18-month and 12-month service periods of some NATO conscript armies). Generally speaking, it has also had better equipment sooner than the NATO armies. Another advantage, which could well be decisive, is that the overwhelming predominance of power in the Warsaw Pact is held by a single army with one system of supply, one tactical doctrine, and one type of equipment. Just how large a price in fighting capacity the NATO powers would pay for the fact that they are an alliance with only very partial integration could only be discovered in the event of war. But it would be a high price.

This Soviet predominance is, however, primarily in the potential of the Soviet Army. The forces maintained in East Germany, Poland and Hungary are not decisively stronger than the front-line NATO forces which are maintained in Germany. The Soviet Army's superiority is concentrated in its reserves.

Why is so much power maintained at so much expense after so many years of apparent peace? The NATO answer to this is that the Soviets have been prevented from extending their control across Western Europe by the obvious capacity of the alliance to meet Soviet forces on the ground and to hold them while the massive nuclear forces destroy their capacity and will to make war. This has been NATO doctrine for many years; and the alliance has shown no disposition to change it. Most NATO governments would agree that the Soviet Union is probably not aggressive in Europe. But they would argue that the reason for this is that the Soviets have been deterred by the alliance from further adventuring. In particular, it is the alliance conventional defence in Europe which ensures that the Americans are fully committed to every action which is taken in a crisis. The presence of such external powers as Britain and Canada means that the continuing American presence is easier and that there is a natural and inevitable unity of the West in the face of any European threat. Strong American forces in Germany are desired both by those who believe in the nuclear deterrent and by those who want a conventional defence. For the deterrent school, they are the presence which guarantees the use of the heavy nuclear forces; for the conventional school, they are the essential means of defending Western Europe.

Opposition to the commitment in Germany has therefore come less from military or strategic thinkers than from those who are concerned with cost. For many years, Britain, in particular, has felt the pressure on her foreign exchange resources of maintaining forces in Germany. After 1960, the United States found its long period of surplus with the rest of the world was coming to an end. It too began to worry about the weight on its balance of payments, though the German Government has made a considerable effort to balance this through arms buying in the United States. As long as the financial situation is kept in balance in this way, the main challenge to the American efforts in Germany will be from competing demands for troops else-where. This depends on developments in Asia and Latin America.

The Soviet forces in Germany reflect the profound con-viction of successive Soviet Governments that the Western powers are naturally aggressive and are determined if pos-sible to destroy Communism. Soviet opinion has always been especially hostile to the Federal Republic of Germany on the ground that the West Germans are determined to reunify their country. In the period of the American atomic monopoly (effectively, until about 1953), the Soviets sought to maintain an overwhelming predominance in force in Central Europe. More recently, as they have achieved a substantial capacity to deter the use of the West's nuclear weapons, they have allowed things to move more towards equality.

Virtually all opinion on both sides has therefore been agreed about the importance of maintaining an effective defensive capacity, but this has left the military planners with the unanswered question : What kind of war are we supposed to be ready to fight?

The best known attempt to produce a coherent answer to this is the MC-70 plan which NATO produced in 1957. No doubt there is a comparable Soviet master plan. MC-70 was intended to provide working answers to the basic questions. It said that NATO ought to have thirty divi-sions on the ground in Central Europe continually ready to fight; and it ought to be able to bring these up to sixty after a period of time. Stocks should be adequate to main-tain the forces in battle for ninety days; and the troops should be equipped and organized to fight either with or without tactical nuclear weapons. From the start, a num-ber of armies—the British, the Belgian, the Dutch, the French—regarded this as a counsel of perfection which could not and would not be met. As a result, the stocks for the different NATO armies are designed to keep them fighting for periods which vary from thirty to ninety days.

The greatest uncertainty was and is the place of tactical nuclear weapons in any defence of Western Europe. These weapons have been stockpiled in large numbers with the armies and air forces of the NATO powers. Altogether, there are now many thousands, all of which were built in the United States; and they are maintained under the physical control of American servicemen. The other NATO allies own and operate vehicles which are to deliver them but not the explosives themselves.

The reason for the uncertainty about tactical nuclear weapons is that military commanders and the NATO planners have very little idea about when they would and would not be allowed to use these weapons. Recent American presidents, at least, have been very reluctant to give freedom of choice on an overwhelmingly political question like the use of nuclear weapons to military commanders—especially to commanders who might resort to them to avoid a local defeat. It is now generally accepted that a decision to use nuclear weapons in a European situation will not be taken at a military level : and that this will apply not just to the first use but to every use. Close political control has been established and this has been given a technical basis with the introduction of electronic release mechanisms. These allow the political authorities, in effect, to hold the key to these weapons in their own hands if they choose. Or they may place the key at some point in their chain of command.

The inevitable uncertainties in all this make military planning very difficult. Those who must provide the organization, doctrine and equipment must know if they are going to be expected to fight a long battle without the use of nuclear weapons. In that case, they will organize their forces differently and will give them for example, much more conventional artillery. NATO has revealed the stages of its own thought by taking out much of its heavy and medium artillery and then bringing it back. The decision to return to this kind of firepower was a strong indication that tactical nuclear weapons were being given a lower priority. On the other hand, there has been a 100 per cent increase in the actual numbers of these weapons stock-piled on the soil of Western Europe over the last few years.

A fundamental NATO difficulty is that it has so little depth in which to defend itself. The great retreat which the Soviet army conducted in the face of the Hitler attack could not be repeated in Western Europe. There simply is not the space. There are also strong political objections from those who might be overrun. Stalin was not dealing with an independent Ukrainian Government.

Military thinking in the early 1950s was that it would be necessary to retreat to the Pyrenees and the English Channel while the effect of atomic bombing of the Soviet Union did its work. Later, substantial force goals were established to make possible a defence on the great natural barrier of the Rhine. This was more acceptable to French opinion; but with the entry of West Germany into NATO in 1954 it was necessary to reconsider this. The alliance then decided to adapt itself to a completely forward stra-tegy. Rather than fight for ultimate victory, it would hold ground at all costs. With cities like Hamburg so close to the Soviet lines, it was argued that the central problem was to prevent the Soviets from taking any territory at all. An armistice was likely to be made on a ceasefire line. Any war which was not to be suicidal would have to be short; and a forward defence was therefore essential. Military opinion, thinking in terms of an effective general defence of Western Europe, could see strong objections to this; but the facts of German politics and the apparent realities of nuclear war left no alternative.

Soviet doctrine for the defence of Eastern Europe is not known. It is presumed in the West that in any major in-cident the Soviets would have a serious internal security problem on their hands in East Germany, Poland and Hun-gary, at least; and that this is an important element in restraining the Soviets from challenges which reach the point of physical conflict.

Neither side has ever recognized a need to maintain large-scale forces outside the Central Area. Northern Norway is lightly held by the small Norwegian armed forces. In the south, Italy, Greece and Turkey have substantial forces under arms and the United States maintains substantial supporting naval airpower in its Mediterranean Sixth Fleet; but these forces do not compare in power and weight to those in and around Germany.

It is clear that the whole problem of European defence on both sides of the East-West Line is one of choice in the event of a crisis. Both sides know the vast strategic forces arrayed against them, but they do not know in what circumstances (if any) they might be used and in what way; both know of the great numbers of battlefield nuclear weapons of various kinds, but they do not know in what circumstances they might be released to the troops for use; and both know that substantial and highly mobile conventional forces are capable of deep penetrations into their territory from the other side. Any conflict would be a matter of constant choice and judgment among these facts. There is no obvious course which a European war might follow. It would be determined by those who must take the decisions in a crisis.

NATO has the profound problem of acting together as an alliance if a crisis or war situation developed. Its main attempt to deal with this is its common command structures which are designed to enable it to fight as a unit. The main NATO powers (the United States, Britain, France and Germany) have also tried to come to terms with a single major crisis situation—that of Berlin. During the Berlin crisis of 1961, they set up planning groups which tried to anticipate every possible move by the Soviets and to find countermeasures which would have the effect of deterring short of larger war. The results of this are, of course, secret; but it is known that a wide measure of agreement was reached from positions which were at first very different.

Berlin and Germany lie at the heart of the most dangerous but also the most tried and tested dispute in the world. Fundamentally, the dispute is about the future of Germany, and especially of East Germany. The NATO powers do not recognize the German Democratic Republic and consider that Germany has a right to be unified under institutions of her own choice. The Soviets want the 1945 settlement to be made permanent on the basis of some kind of confederation of Germany. Around this dispute there has gathered a high proportion of the world's force. But after years of trying each other's will and capacity, the two sides seem to have found a military balance which they prefer not to tamper with. There is no sign—in spite of the 2,000,000 troops, the thousands of tactical nuclear weapons and the strategic armouries—that either side of Europe now thinks itself insecure.

CHAPTER V

DOCTRINES OF WAR

Thousands of nuclear weapons exist in the hands of four powers. The Russians and Americans could destroy each other's civil societies on the order of one man or of a very few men. Britain could do massive damage. France has her first batch of atomic bombs. In addition to the strategic nuclear forces, there are many thousands of nuclear weapons designed for tactical purposes: battlefield bombardment, anti-aircraft, depth charges, and so on. Behind these, there must now be huge stocks of fabricated atomic and thermo-nuclear bombs which can be brought forward at any time if the delivery means can be found for them. The official American view of this has been summed up in formal Congressional testimony by Mr Robert McNamara, the Secretary of Defense:

'Even if the Soviets in the 1970 period were to assign their entire available missile force to attacks on our strategic missiles (reserving only refire missiles and bomber-delivered weapons for urban targets), our analysis shows that a very large proportion of our alert forces would still survive. ... It is clear, therefore, that our strategic offensive forces are far more than adequate to inflict unacceptable damage on the Soviet Union, even after absorbing a well-coordinated Soviet first strike against those forces. Indeed, it appears that even a relatively small proportion of these forces would furnish us with a completely adequate deterrent to deliberate Soviet nuclear attack on the United States or its allies.'

He also, however, made the following statement at the same time :

'Against the forces we expect the Soviets to have during the next decade, it will be virtually impossible for us to be able to ensure anything approaching complete protection for our population, no matter how large the general war forces we were to provide, including even the hypothetical possibility of striking first. . . . The Soviets have the technical and economic capability to prevent us from achieving a posture which could keep our fatalities below some tens of millions.'

It is unlikely that the Soviet Defence Minister would differ very much from this statement. Nor would any other government. The question about these forces is not their capacity to destroy cities and indeed whole populations. It is the effect which the ability to wreak total destruction has on the relations of states.

And this reduces itself to the primary question : In what circumstances might such forces be used? And the secondary question : In what circumstances might one side think there was a real danger that the other would use his nuclear forces? History gives us some guidance in this matter. The United States (with Britain and Canada) used atomic bombs twice against Japanese cities. At that time, she was engaged in an all-out war in which she had vowed to achieve the unconditional surrender of her enemy. This was going to cost many thousands of casualties in conquering the Japanese islands. At the same time, she knew there was no danger of retaliation. The Japanese obviously did not have atomic weapons; nor did they have a delivery system able to reach American cities.

The Korean War makes a sharp contrast. At that time, the United States monopoly had just been broken but the Soviet Union could not have had a large stock of weapons. It also lacked a delivery system able to reach the United States. Yet, so far as is known, the Truman Government did not give serious consideration to using nuclear explosives in spite of casualties which were greater than American casualties in the First World War. So with other major conflicts like the Vietnam War or the British confrontation with Indonesia on behalf of Malaysia. The only exception to this was the determination of President Eisenhower on taking office in 1953 that if a Korean armistice was not signed nuclear weapons would have to be used against Chinese bases.

On the other hand, it would be quite wrong to suggest that their existence has had no effect on governments. They have influenced almost every use of power, especially where dealings with other nuclear powers are concerned. In the long arduous East-West struggle in Europe, hardly a shot has been fired. Both sides have avoided any kind of conflict which might draw them to the point where they could see no alternative to using nuclear weapons. The fear of escalation up to the use of nuclear weapons has become the central fear : and the threat of escalation has become a prime means of compelling an opponent to settle. The most telling example of this was undoubtedly the Cuban missile crisis, where both sides knew that they must find a settlement but each was anxious to find it at a point which was favourable to its interests.

Those who think about this problem are inclined to come to the conclusion that nuclear weapons are uniquely able to deter an enemy but are a most unsatisfactory form of defence. This has led governments to emphasize their dependence on nuclear weapons to the maximum in their public statements and public position while trying to minimize this dependence in their military planning. The most famous American example of the military threat was the so-called 'massive retaliation' statement of Mr John Foster Dulles, then Secretary of State, in January, 1954 :

'The President and the National Security Council have taken a basic decision to depend primarily upon a great capacity to retaliate instantly by means and at places of our own choosing.'

Statements along these lines have been much more common from British Governments. In the 1966 Defence Review, for example, the Government said :

'Once nuclear weapons were employed in Europe, on however limited a scale, it is almost certain that, unless the aggressor quickly decided to stop fighting, the conflict would escalate rapidly to a general nuclear exchange.'

The Soviets, too, have repeatedly emphasized the impossibility of limited war. A typical statement is the following : 'One of the most important concepts of Soviet military doctrine is that a world war, if it is unleashed by the imperialists, unavoidably must assume the character of a nuclear missile war—a war in which the primary means of destruction will be nuclear weapons and the primary means of delivering them to the target will be missiles. The massive use of atomic and thermo-nuclear weapons, with unlimited potential for delivering them to any target in a matter of minutes by using missiles, will make it possible rapidly to achieve the maximum military results at any distance and over enormous areas. It should be emphasized that, given international relations as they are under the present level of development in military technology, an armed conflict will inevitably develop into an all-out nuclear war, if nuclear powers are drawn into it.'[1]

Statements of this kind are intended to encourage caution on the other side. It remains open, however, just at what stage governments would commit acts which can only be described as suicidal. Those who have thought about these problems have sought ways of acting which would constantly renew and reinforce the deterrent effect of strategic nuclear power without ever being placed in the position where it had to be used on an uncontrollable scale. They realize that a country which is bluffing might have its bluff called : so they cannot afford to bluff. But equally they do not want to commit suicide. So if driven to the

---

[1] Sokolovsky (ed.), op. cit., p. 189.

brink, they would take action which would make it clear that they were still mounting a serious threat with their nuclear weapons. In a situation like this, they would not be primarily concerned with doing damage : they would be concerned with showing that their deterrent really existed.

Probably the only statement by the government of a nuclear power which has openly suggested that something other than massive retaliation might be the policy in general war was Mr McNamara's Ann Arbor speech in the spring of 1962. In a celebrated passage from this, he said :

'The United States has come to the conclusion that to the extent feasible, basic military strategy in a possible general nuclear war should be approached in much the same way that more conventional military operations have been regarded in the past. That is to say, principal military objectives, in the event of a nuclear war stemming from a major attack on the Alliance, should be the destruction of the enemy's military forces, not of his civilian population.'

It is significant that this sort of thing has not been said again. But those who know Mr McNamara's thought and that of his advisers do not doubt that this remains his policy. In one form or another, it is probably the policy of all nuclear powers. They will always seek some way out of a tense situation short of suicide. But it is interesting that when the United States became convinced only six months after the Ann Arbor speech that the Soviet Union was secretly introducing offensive missiles into Cuba (contrary to the solemn assurances of representatives of the Soviet Government) it adopted what looked very much more like the traditional declaratory policy. President Kennedy was obviously very fearful of a situation in which the Soviets let the Cuban Government get control of nuclear weapons. At the outset of the Cuban missile crisis, he made this public statement : 'It shall be the policy of this nation to regard any nuclear missile launched from Cuba against any nation in the Western Hemisphere as an attack by the Soviet

Union on the United States, requiring *a full retaliatory response*[1] on the Soviet Union.' Only a few months after the Ann Arbor speech, the need to take an extreme declaratory position had obviously reasserted itself.

If it is recognized that the problem which faces governments is to find ways of responding which are both effective and non-suicidal, there is still a wide variety of possible choices. These, of course, depend on the weapons that exist : and this is how strategic thinking and weapons procurement have become inextricably bound up. Some people feel that what is needed above all is the ability to have local dominance in all situations without using nuclear weapons. They point out that the Americans were able to impose their naval dominance over Soviet ships off Cuba and so force the Soviets to resort to nuclear weapons or withdraw. While few would dispute the advantage which local dominance gives, others point out that the Western powers, for example, have little hope of this in Europe and especially in Berlin, where the Soviets are obviously predominant. They argue that it is probably essential to find ways to do serious damage without becoming involved in an all-out nuclear war.

Here there has been a lengthy argument in the United States between those who wanted to be in a position to destroy Soviet nuclear forces and those who thought the ability to do this would itself be dangerous. This was known as the argument about counterforce—that is, the ability to destroy forces. Those who favoured it said that to be able to destroy Soviet nuclear forces in a crisis would be a most effective deterrent without being suicidal : and that the effect would be to reduce the damage that would be done in a nuclear war. Their opponents said that a Soviet Government knowing that its forces could be destroyed would use them rather than have this happen. They would be forced to be trigger happy in a crisis. The Ann Arbor speech and the general line of Mr McNamara's de-

[1] Italics inserted.

fence testimony suggests that the counterforce party has had a qualified victory. The United States armed forces have been built to achieve the maximum damage limitation—and that means the ability to destroy Soviet forces on the ground. But the American Government always goes out of its way to insist that nothing it can do can possibly bring it to the point where it could avoid millions of American casualties in a major war. If it did claim to be in this position, the Soviets would have to conclude that they were not in a stable situation. A vulnerable nuclear power is a tense one and one which may think the only course open to it is to attack first. Official American statements reflect a recognition of this.

This thinking about the best way to conduct a nuclear crisis has not been popular with America's European allies. The British, French and German governments have all in their differing ways resisted speculation about how a major crisis should be conducted. They have refused to accept the prospect that nuclear weapons might be used without bringing on a massive nuclear exchange. They have preferred to insist that chaos would inevitably ensue and at best the results would be unpredictable and uncontrollable. Neither the British nor the French government has tried to furnish itself with deep underground or airborne control arrangements. The German Government can foresee nothing but total national calamity if nuclear weapons are used at all : and they therefore resent any suggestion that more limited forms of war may prove possible. They insist on the deterrent which exists and can be seen to exist and can only be undermined—with possibly catastrophic consequences—by any suggestion that there may be hesitation in resorting to it.

Some opinion, especially in France, has felt that the function of the small Western European nuclear forces is to add additional assurance to the American deterrent. It has been argued that the British and French governments are in a position to introduce nuclear weapons

D

into a conflict when the Americans may be anxious to keep them out. The fact that they can do this increases the effectiveness of the deterrent.

Both the British and French nuclear forces have been designed primarily to be able to strike against Soviet cities. They are relatively small numerically : and they fit into a simple doctrine of deterrence. The British force has been defended less as a trigger to the American forces than as a force which could, if necessary, deter the Soviet Union independently. It is not claimed that it could in any way fight equally against the Soviets; the argument is that it could do so much damage to the Soviet Union that the Soviets would never act in such a way as to bring it into action.

The Soviet Union is clearly closer to the Anglo-French view of limitation in nuclear war than it is to the American position. The Soviet government has avoided all reference to limited nuclear war. All statements on general war have the same emphasis as British or French statements : they insist on the inevitability of chaos, the uncontrollability of the situation which would result, and the very small chance that there would be of avoiding a cataclysm. If they have built secure command posts to keep control even after a nuclear attack has taken place, they have not publicised the fact.

But underlying the Soviet position is a much more orthodox soldiers' view of war. The Soviets did not engage in strategic bombing of Nazi Germany on any scale : and they believe in their hearts that the decisive thing is to hold ground. They have been very reluctant to see even nuclear war as anything but a larger arena in which the struggle for the control of the decisive territory would go on. That is why they were so perplexed by the apparent position of the West in the early 1950s. The Western powers seemed to have put themselves in a position to launch nuclear retaliation without being able to stop the Soviet armies or invade the Soviet Union.

The argument about when nuclear weapons can be used has dominated all military thought and planning in Europe and North America for about fifteen years. There has always been a 'tripwire' school of opinion which has insisted that all that was needed to secure Western Europe from the Soviets (and no doubt Eastern Europe from the NATO powers) was a light force which could make sure that any enemy attack was determined and genuine. There has also been the landpower school which has said that nothing less than a full capacity to defend would do. Into this has been fitted, with great uncertainty, the idea of using nuclear weapons locally to stop an aggressor or to destroy his supply lines.

This issue has never been satisfactorily worked out. Governments have not been able to see their way clearly. In the face of a crisis, they increase their conventional power and their nuclear threats. In the end, both sides have obviously decided that there are severe limits on what 'the deterrent' can be relied on to do. Both have chosen to maintain very large non-nuclear forces at colossal and increasing expense. Yet neither has maintained anything like an effective wartime non-nuclear establishment.

The vast nuclear forces are there and they impose themselves dramatically on any crisis involving the major powers on opposite sides. But they have only cast their shadow over other forms of power. They have not, in the end, replaced them.

CHAPTER VI

ALLIANCE STRAINS

Although the strategic nuclear weapons point at America and Russia across the Arctic and Canada, the central power confrontation in the world is still clearly in Europe. While the Americans and Russians may be the main contenders on each side, this is a challenge of alliance to alliance, not of one power to another. But what, in reality, are NATO and the Warsaw Pact? What do they undertake to do and how much of it can they accomplish? What are their limits?

There can be no doubt that the North Atlantic Treaty Organization is the largest and most ambitious alliance structure in history. It reflects the way in which the American, British, Canadians, Free French and other allies fought their successful campaign against Germany in 1944-5. Supreme commands were set up to plan and fight the common enemy in Europe and for the war against Japan; and when Czechoslovakia had fallen to the Communists and South Korea was suddenly invaded from North Korea, it was felt by the NATO countries that there would be no time to organize common commands for war if an invasion of this kind was launched in Europe. With the speed at which aggressors might be able to move over the ground, the wartime organization would need to be ready in times of peace. The man who had been allied Supreme Commander in Europe in the Second World War, General Eisenhower, became the first NATO Supreme Commander for Europe. He and his successors have been simultaneously Commander-in-Chief of American forces in Europe and Supreme Allied Commander, Europe. A parallel supreme Atlantic Command was given to the commander of the American Atlantic Fleet in Norfolk, Virginia. Under these two commanders, an elaborate series of land, sea and air commands was established to plan in peace and command in war the forces which the alliance had created for its defence.

The NATO countries also established a Council which had the control of its supreme commanders. This body has ambassadors from each of the member countries and takes its decisions by unanimity. Thus, no member of the alliance can be compelled by his membership in the alliance to do anything against his will. The obligation which all undertake is to treat an attack on any one as if it had been an attack on themselves and to take what measures they consider necessary to repel it. These measures remain a matter of individual decision by governments.

The NATO commands are therefore obliged to make ready to fight a war on the assumption that all members of the alliance will have agreed to fight as one. Obviously, the common planners cannot question the assumption that all will act together. They are also obliged to maintain a fairly simple notion of the kind of war they might be called on to fight. While the Americans, and to a lesser extent others, have become more concerned with the problems of crisis management rather than war, and local challenges rather than all-out war, NATO has had difficulty in abandoning the old vision of the all-out Russian attack on the lines of the North Korean attack on South Korea. Anything else is too complicated and too political for common military commands.

To this has been added another profound difficulty. From the start, the United States Government declined to involve its strategic nuclear forces in the NATO organization. The Strategic Air Command was organized with its headquarters at Omaha, Nebraska, outside the NATO structure. When the British developed a strategic air force, this too was kept outside NATO and British officers did their common planning with the Americans at Omaha. In 1963, the British Government committed RAF Bomber Command to NATO and the Americans committed three of their Polaris-firing submarines; but the main strategic forces which NATO doctrine says would be the decisive forces in a European war have remained in purely American hands.

Some efforts have been made to remedy this situation in recent years. NATO is now represented at the Joint Strategic Target Planning organization which the Americans have established to co-ordinate their Navy and Air Force strategic weapons. The organization selects particular targets related to its role to be covered and these are assigned to particular forces. This no doubt helps to reassure those who feel entirely out of touch with these things that plans for general war do not run contrary to their national interest. But it is not the target lists that matter; it is the decisions which are taken in particular situations. No government can anticipate how it will act in a crisis. So participation in the most intimate planning processes does not in the end leave the ally very much wiser.

But NATO has deeper troubles than this. The alliance was originally organized, in effect, by the Americans and British; and each American Supreme Commander had a British deputy. The French were in a third position which became increasingly uncomfortable. Their dissatisfaction was more strongly expressed when General de Gaulle took power in 1958 and was rebuffed in his proposal that the alliance should be organized around a three-power directorate of America, Britain and France. Throughout the Berlin crises of the early 1960s he took very little further action; but in the more peaceable days of 1966 he announced his intention of withdrawing from the military command structure of NATO while remaining a party to the

Treaty. This development makes any plans to provide a general ground defence of Western Europe very difficult to put into military practice. France is the essential rear area to any effective defence of Germany. But as NATO was never entirely clear about whether it had to be ready to fight such a war it has not been paralysed by this French decision.

The other large power in NATO, West Germany, has provided a different series of problems for the alliance : and on the whole the alliance has had no more success in solving these. The German government has been preoccupied for some years by the problem of nuclear guarantees. Having pledged itself in 1954 not to manufacture nuclear weapons on its own soil, the federal government has been anxious to know that it had a strong and enduring guarantee that any threat to its security would be permanently deterred. More specifically, the German defence planners have been concerned that there is a large force of 700 Soviet rockets apparently trained on to Western Europe and there is nothing in Europe to match them. This concern has been shared by the NATO European headquarters which has argued for many years that an equivalent NATO weapon should be developed. The United States was for a time developing such a weapon to meet this type of requirement but it has been cancelled.

In the course of this general debate about the control of nuclear forces, the American Government decided to sponsor the formation of a multilateral force, as it was called, of strategic nuclear weapons which would be jointly owned and operated by a number of countries, including Germany. The American hope was that this might lead ultimately to a European force from which the United States itself might withdraw. It was proposed that this should be seaborne because of the political complications of basing it on land. The Polaris missile was therefore considered to be ideal for it : but after going through various phases the Americans proposed that international manning of submarines would be difficult. They therefore settled on a proposal for twenty-five surface ships each to carry eight Polaris missiles —a total force of 200 missiles.

This idea was strongly opposed by the Soviet Union, which considered that any plan designed to satisfy the nuclear ambitions of the German Government must in the nature of things be transferring some element of nuclear control : otherwise, what satisfaction would it provide? It was also extremely unpopular with the French Government, which considered it an attempt to extend American control into Europe and to undermine the nuclear independence of France. The Scandinavian members of NATO, Norway and Denmark, have always had a strong non-nuclear policy and announced their intention of staying out. Because the Americans saw this as a European arrangement, Canada dropped out at an early stage. The Dutch were hesitant about the expense and the Italians were anxious to participate only if the British joined in. As a result, the possibility that the MLF might be anything more than an American-German force was soon seen to depend on the attitude of the British Government.

In the midst of the MLF debate of 1964, the Labour Party took power in Britain. Its leaders had been strongly critical of the MLF on the grounds that it seemed to involve some kind of spread of nuclear weapons from one country to another. A British plan, under the name of Atlantic Nuclear Force, or ANF, was produced : this included the commitment of nuclear forces from Britain, France and the United States to a common force and had a mixed-manned component which would presumably be the same Polaris-carrying surface ships as were being proposed by the Americans, though in smaller numbers. The essence of the British position was that the United States, Britain and anyone else who wanted it would have a permanent right of veto over any use of the force. In this way, the British argued, there could be no question of any changed control over nuclear weapons.

The German Government did not like the British plan. Nor, for that matter, did the Russians or the French. But its main effect was to give the British a position from which to oppose the MLF without coming into open conflict with the American Government. In these circumstances, President Johnson decided that the opposition to the plan was too widespread to make it realistic. He dissolved the large project office which had been formed and an experimental mixed manned ship, the USS Claude Ricketts, was quietly paid off.

This clumsy failure of alliance left the nuclear problem unresolved and even undefined. American and British opinion began to move towards the need to provide for more knowledge and consultation; but German official opinion remained convinced that it was desirable that the long-term commitment of alliance should take the form of some tangible force. In the jargon, they would still like a hardware solution.

In this growing atmosphere of uncertainty, the NATO treaty is approaching the end of its twenty years of guaranteed life. It was signed in 1949 and became binding on the members for this period : after that, each could withdraw by giving a year's notice. But underlying the formal alliance problem is a range of political uncertainties deriving from the apparent decline of Soviet ambition to dominate Western Europe; the possible growth of close relations between the main NATO members and the Soviet Union; and, above all, the long-term relationship which America will have with Europe (if it unites politically) or with Britain, France and Germany.

The Warsaw Pact is not at all like NATO. The NATO problem is one of finding a way for substantial powers to work together. The heart of NATO's troubles has been the American relationship with France and Germany. Whether or not the members of the Warsaw Pact are all satellites of the Soviet Union, none of them is a substantial power in his own right. In the early years of the Pact, they were entirely subservient to Soviet policy in every sphere. More recently, they have at times adopted a cautiously independent line. One reason for this is that the Sino-Soviet split has created a position within the Communist movement in which loyalty to Communism and support for Russian policy are no longer necessarily identical.

The effect of these alliances in Europe is to confirm the forward positions of the American, British and Russian forces which were established in 1945. This is not a simple matter of manning a line. In Austria, for example, there are no foreign forces and a doctrine of neutralization covers the country. So in another sense with Yugoslavia which has carved out its own version of Communist neutrality. In Scandinavia, the subtle shadings of Finnish friendship to the Soviets, Swedish armed neutrality and Norwegian membership of NATO with no foreign forces on Norwegian soil produce a situation which is very far from an East-West confrontation. But in Germany, the decisive area, the alliance structures have kept the great powers on the lines they occupied under the Potsdam Agreement of 1945. The territory on both sides is saturated with power on a scale unknown to history. In addition to the million highly equipped soldiers which are maintained there, every sentry on the Berlin Wall is linked by some unknown process of escalation to the possible destruction of all mankind. The stakes on this table have been set so high that (so it is hoped) no-one dares to gamble. When Mr Khrushchev was tempted even by the apparently favourable odds of his Berlin position, he soon decided that the risk of losing remained too high.

It may be that any conflict anywhere could bring into play the forces of unbelievable destruction which stand permanently ready for use. But in Germany the direct links are visible through the headquarters, the treaties, the foreign armies, the promises and the plans of twenty years. This has imposed severe restraint on both sides. The Soviets protested bitterly at the rearmament of West Germany, but had to recognize the freedom of action of the West on their side of the Potsdam frontier. Equally, the West stood by while the revolutionary Hungarian regime was destroyed by Soviet action and while the Berlin Wall split a great city down its centre.

Eastern and Western Europe are deeply involved in each other's lives, and will be increasingly over the years. A new political relationship might ultimately arise. But for the present each side has freedom to operate on its own side of the Potsdam line : and the greatest power concentration in the world is thought to be among the most stable because this rule of action has been reluctantly accepted by all concerned.

CHAPTER VII

CRISIS MANAGEMENT

We know that these vast strategic and tactical forces exist. But we do not know when or how they might be used. Nevertheless, there is some evidence about what will happen in a challenge by the Soviet Union to the United States and her allies. We have real cases which we can examine. Backed by the ultimate consequence of war and possible annihilation, the greatest powers have already found themselves compelled to bargain over important issues. They have given the impression that they were moving close to the brink; and they have finally found their way to a settlement without war. The two most striking recent examples are the Berlin crisis of 1961, which finally petered out in 1964; and the Cuban missile crisis of 1962, which lasted four weeks.

Both these crises began with a direct conflict between the objectives of the two sides. They went through similar stages : positions were stated; tension grew; moves were made which committed each side to its position and helped to show determination; the danger increased; the possible lines along which a bargain might be struck began to emerge; and finally the bargain was struck and the situation dissolved.

1.

The Berlin crisis of 1961 formed part of the long dispute about the status of Berlin which went back to the end of the Second World War. The Soviet Union had withdrawn from the four-power administration of the city, leaving the western zones of Berlin as an island deep inside the territory of East Germany. The United States, Britain and France insisted that the rights of the Western powers in West Berlin and on the access routes to the city derived from the surrender of the German Reich. These could only be changed by a peace treaty signed by all the belligerents. The Western powers consistently refused to recognize the government of the German Democratic Republic as in any way legitimate. The Soviets wanted two Germanies united in some form of confederation. The Western powers insisted that only a truly reunified Germany exercising self-determination through free elections would be acceptable. This was the old-established debate.

In 1958, the Soviet government developed a new approach to the Berlin question. It suggested that the western part of Berlin should become 'a demilitarized free city within the structure of the State in whose territory it lies'. It might have its own government and direct its own economy, but it would have to undertake not to permit on its territory 'any hostile or subversive activity'. It was this objective which Mr Khrushchev decided to achieve in 1961.

His first major move was made at his meeting with the new American President, John F. Kennedy, at Vienna in June, 1961. He handed Mr Kennedy a memorandum which asked for a German peace treaty within a definite period after which all the occupation rights would disappear. This was an old proposal, but the memorandum spelled out the threat in unmistakeable terms :

'If the United States does not show an understanding of the necessity of concluding a peace treaty, we shall regret this, since we would have to sign a peace treaty, which it would be impossible and dangerous to delay further, not with all States, but only with those that want to sign it.

'The peace treaty will specifically record the status of West Berlin as a free city. . . . At the same time this will also mean the liquidation of the occupation regime in West Berlin with all the consequences arising therefrom. Specifically, the question of using land, water and air communications across the territory of the German Democratic Republic will have to be settled not otherwise than through appropriate agreements with the German Democratic Republic.'

The wording of this was therefore quite specific on two points : 1. effective Western forces would disappear from Berlin (though Mr Khrushchev was prepared to agree to token contingents, including Russians and neutrals, in West Berlin); 2. the city would be dependent on East Germany for all rights of access and none of these rights would belong to the United States, Britain and France.

This situation had the advantage for the Soviets that it gave them the full initiative. They could sign any peace treaty they chose with the East Germans at any time they chose. All the West could do was to insist that they did not accept the consequences of any such action and would not deal with the East Germans.

In a broadcast to the American people, Mr Kennedy stated his reply publicly :

'I made it clear to Mr Khrushchev that the security of Western Europe and therefore our own security, are deeply involved in our presence and our access rights to West Berlin, that these rights are based on law and not on sufferance and that we are determined to maintain these rights at any risk and thus meet our obligation to the people of West Berlin and their right to choose their own future.'

The battle lines were thus set. Mr Khrushchev then removed the doubt about timing with a television broadcast on June 15 : 'The conclusion of a peace treaty with Germany cannot be postponed any longer,' he said. 'A peace settlement in Europe must be attained this year.' The same day, Herr Ulbricht, the East German Head of State, said that after the conclusion of the peace treaty people travelling between Berlin and the Federal Republic by water, land or air 'will be subject to our control, for these are our communications'. Mr Khrushchev said he was stopping the announced reductions in the Soviet armed forces and increasing military spending. They would 'rebuff the aggressive forces if they decide to frustrate peaceful settlement by force of arms'.

A formal rejection of the Soviet proposals for a peace treaty was made by the US, Britain and France on July 17 in Notes to Moscow. The American Note said : 'A "peace treaty" with the part of Germany's territory termed "German Democratic Republic" by the Soviet Government could have no validity in international law, nor could it affect in any way whatsoever the rights of the Western Powers.' The British said : 'If the Soviet Government puts its declared intentions into effect, this would indeed lead to a most serious situation.'

The development of the crisis still remained entirely in Soviet hands, though the Western powers had begun an exhaustive study of the counter measures they might take. During August, three major Soviet moves were made. On August 13, the Soviet sector of Berlin was sealed off from the western sectors by barricades erected overnight. For the first time, the city was simply cut down the middle and this was reinforced by the construction of a wall. The first physical show of determination by the West followed five days later. An American battle group of 1,500 men was ordered down the Helmstedt-Berlin *autobahn* and the British reinforced their garrison with thirty-four additional armoured vehicles. The Vice-President of the United States, Mr Lyndon Johnson, was in Berlin on August 19 to greet the troops.

Three days later, a Soviet note accused the West of breaking the old four power agreements in the way they were using the air routes to and from Berlin. This could only be understood as a strong suggestion that even the air corridors might soon be subject to attack. Eight days after this, on August 31, the Soviets reversed their promise two years earlier that they would not test nuclear weapons unless the Western powers did. They embarked on a large scale programme which involved a total of forty tests in two months, including the vast 57-megaton device.

Planners from the United States, Britain, France and West Germany worked on answers to every possible move the Soviets might make. The deadline of the end of the year came closer and it was clear that someone was going to have to give ground soon. In fact, it was the Soviet Union. Mr Khrushchev simply lifted the time limit in the course of his speech to the 22nd Congress of the Soviet Communist Party in Moscow in mid-October. Although this suggested that he was anxious not to have to back up his threats, he had by no means given up.

Harassment of air travel on the corridors began in February and March of 1962. Large numbers of extra Soviet flights were made and Soviet fighters began to buzz Western transport aircraft. Metal strips were dropped to confuse navigation and air traffic control. In May and June, tension rose in Berlin with the shooting of refugees; and feelings reached their height in August when a young refugee, Peter Fechter, was shot by East German police and allowed to bleed to death on the Communist side of what was by then the Berlin Wall in full view of West Berliners. The popular protest was strong. The guard for the Soviet War Memorial in the British Sector was stoned for three consecutive nights. The Soviets then made the apparently dangerous move of abolishing the Commandant's office of the Soviet garrison : but they avoided the worst risks by leaving its functions with the Soviet armed forces in Germany.

By this time, however, the failure of the Soviet challenge had become clear to everyone concerned. The Western powers had not moved on their basic position. The Soviets were prepared to do everything short of war; but they drew back at the prospect of starting something the end of which no-one could predict. The end of the challenge began to come into sight. President Kennedy visited Berlin in June, 1963. There was a spate of incidents on the *autobahn* during October and November, 1963, in which the Western powers showed their solidarity and fidelity to the post-war agreements. But in June, 1964, the Soviets signed a different kind of treaty with East Germany from the one they had proposed—a treaty of Friendship, Mutual Assistance and Co-operation with East Germany, and it made no mention of Berlin. It seems reasonable to consider this Soviet decision the end of the Berlin crisis. The Soviet challenge had failed completely. Nothing had been gained or lost on either side, though the division of Berlin had been made a physical fact to match the division of Germany.

2.

The Cuban missile crisis followed a simpler and more dramatic course than the Berlin crisis. It brought the world startlingly to the brink of war : and since it was about nuclear weapons it seemed to make the prospect of their use somehow more certain. On the other hand, the Soviet and American objectives in Cuba were by no means as certain as they were in Berlin. There is still legitimate dispute about just what the Americans and the Soviets were trying to achieve in the Cuban crisis. In Berlin, there can be no doubt of the Soviet aim and of the fact that it was not achieved.

The facts of the Cuban situation are that on July 2, 1962, the Cuban Minister of the Armed Forces, Raul Castro, visited Moscow. Later that month a substantial arms build-up began in Cuba; and at the end of August the Americans photographed Soviet surface-to-air guided weapons on Cuban soil. On October 14, a ballistic missile base was photographed at San Cristobal, in Western Cuba, and it rapidly became clear that a substantial build-up of these weapons was in progress.

The Soviet argument has always been that these missiles

were part of a general attempt to give security to Cuba against an American invasion. The American view is that the missiles were introduced into Cuba to damage American prestige in Latin America and to give the Soviet Union a substantial increase in strategic nuclear power at low cost. If the Soviets are right and their objective was to increase Cuban security, this was probably achieved. If either or both of the American explanations is right, the Soviet Union had a disastrous failure.

The course taken by the Soviet missile build-up is not in dispute. When presented with the facts, President Kennedy and virtually all of his advisers were in no doubt that the situation was intolerable and unacceptable. Their problem was how to stop and reverse the process, which had already gone a long way.

Assuming that a purely political response was out of the question, the President had three military possibilities open to him : to stop additional Russian ships from reaching Cuba and to try somehow to persuade the Russians to withdraw the missiles which were already there; to bomb the missile sites; or to launch an invasion of Cuba. He had a wide range of options because of the great American superiority on land and sea and in the air in an area just off the United States coast.

Of the three military possibilities, an invasion had the disadvantage that it would take time : and the build-up of the missile force seemed to be going on at a very rapid rate. So a landing, like a policy of doing nothing, was not given much consideration. The debate developed over the relative advantages of bombing the missiles and acting against ships at sea. Bombing the missiles would have the advantage that it would lead rapidly to a complete destruction of those weapons which were already there. But there was a real fear that one or more might be fired against us cities in the course of the operation. The Soviets would probably have substantial casualties unless warning was given and there were hesitations about giving warning. It would also be a politically unpopular operation and might well involve heavy civilian casualties.

Both air attacks and a blockade would be acts of war. Both would involve actions directly against Russians, something which both the Soviets and Americans had been at pains to avoid throughout the Cold War. The advantage of naval action was that it would be discreet, slow in taking effect, and would give the Russian leadership time to consider and react deliberately. It did not exclude a later bombing campaign. This was a decisive argument with President Kennedy and many of his advisers, even though it could achieve only part of the objective.

The naval action was given the name of a quarantine. In revealing the Soviet build-up to the American nation on television, the President committed himself to military action if necessary : 'All ships of any kind bound for Cuba from whatever nation or port will, if found to contain cargoes of offensive weapons, be turned back.' What happened if ships refused to be turned back was not stated; but the implication of the quarantine was that, if necessary, they would have to be sunk.

The tension rose dramatically. To accept would mean humiliation for the Soviets. To leave the ships to be sunk would, in a sense, be a greater humiliation. The submarines in the area would also almost certainly be sunk, even if they managed to find a target or two. The United States would quickly sweep Cuban waters. What would the Soviet do?

The crisis occurred, of course, while the Berlin dispute was still in existence, though in the lull which followed the tension of the summer of 1962. Many believed that the Soviet Union would act in Berlin in retaliation for Cuba. But the Soviets would have no more and no less reason for acting if they were being defeated or humiliated in Cuba. Their objectives in Berlin were clear and comprehensible. They were not looking for an excuse to take Berlin. The fact is that they had failed to find moves which they could make safely. This situation was not altered one way or the other by what happened in or around Cuba.

The one strong card in the Soviets' hand was the fact that much of what they planned to put into Cuba was already there. But the determination which was being shown in Washington inevitably raised the possibility of further measures to achieve the President's objective of ridding Cuba of offensive weapons. (He had, incidentally, committed himself clearly on this point before his Administration first suspected that such weapons might be put into Cuba; and he had constantly reiterated it.)

Whether there were intelligent military options open to the Soviets in Cuba, they were not taken up. They offered instead a political bargain. A Soviet Embassy counsellor, Alexander Fomin, suggested to an American television commentator, John Scali, that the United States should propose that the missile sites be dismantled; that the Cubans should refuse to accept offensive missiles in future; and the United States would undertake not to invade Cuba. At about the same time, a message from Mr Khrushchev said that if the United States gave assurances that it would not attack Cuba (or allow others to attack it), the whole situation would be transformed.

Mr Kennedy wrote to Mr Khrushchev on October 27 that he could agree to two things : (1) the offensive weapons would be removed; (2) the United States and other nations in the Western Hemisphere would 'give assurances against an invasion of Cuba'. On this basis, agreement was rapidly reached. The missiles sailed for home. American strategic missiles on foreign soil—in Italy and Turkey—soon followed them.

The remarkable thing about the Cuban missile crisis was the intensity of the atmosphere of fear and danger and at the same time the almost complete absence of military action. The extremely limited naval action which was ordered was under strict control. It is even said to have led to a bitter exchange between Mr McNamara, representing the Defense Department's doctrine of strict and close control, and the Chief of Naval Operations, Admiral Anderson, who told him that the Navy knew how to carry out an operation of this kind.

The way this crisis developed showed, as Berlin also showed, that in the presence of such vast power the use of force has little function. Armed forces are valuable in so far as they offer options in a crisis which help to convey determination. In a constant series of crises of this kind, troops would probably spend more time being mobilized and demobilized than they would in action. Calling up reserves is a safe but determined move which a government can make when it wants to show its resolve; so is their movement to battle-ready positions; but their use is fraught with danger and uncertainty.

Underlying both crises there was, perhaps, a single factor. This was the failure of American credibility caused by Mr Khrushchev's low opinion of the determination of Mr Kennedy. Whether this was caused by the failure of the Bay of Pigs invasion of Cuba or their meeting in Vienna or both is irrelevant. The balance of terror apparently broke down because one side ceased to respect his opponent. The challenges which followed restored this credibility. The balance of terror can be delicate not just because weapons are vulnerable but also because men miscalculate other men. And both Cuba and Berlin gave the justification for the remark attributed to Mr McNamara : 'There is no such thing these days as strategy : There is only crisis management.'

CHAPTER VIII

CHINA

Every major power is deeply concerned with the future of China. A nation of 700 million vigorous people occupying the centre of a vast continent and dedicated to a revolutionary doctrine is scarcely something which can be ignored.

There are wide differences of view, however, about how urgent the Chinese danger is and what form it will take. At one extreme, the Indian and American governments take the view that China is growing rapidly in power and will pose the main threat to the world order over many years. On the other hand, the general European and Japanese view is that Chinese power is easily overrated and that China's objectives do not on the whole conflict with a reasonable world order. The Soviet Union has gone through a deep disillusionment in its relations with the Communist government of China : but it is probably not yet clear about what relationship it can expect over the long term with its vast southern neighbour.

China has a unique problem of trying to be a major power with a relatively small industrial base. Up to 1960, however, successive Chinese governments had major assistance from great power friends. Nationalist China had close relations with the United States and Communist China was aided on a large scale by the Soviet Union. Both of these friends and allies, however, went through a period of disillusionment. American aid to the Nationalists was cut back after the Marshall mission of 1947 and the Soviet Union suddenly and dramatically withdrew its technicians in 1960. Since then, the armaments industries of China have progressed on their own. No-one doubts that, as with the Soviet Union, these will ultimately become strong and efficient; but with an economy which is still well behind the British economy in industrial production the speed with which this will happen will be dependent on priorities and determination. The co-operation with the Soviet Union up to 1960 has left an important military legacy. Factories for all the main weapons needed for modern infantry are available and can presumably produce the rifles, machine guns and mortars which the Chinese Army needs. Some tanks and medium artillery have been produced in recent years. But in spite of this there is still a shortage of such things as road and rail transport.

The air force was built on Soviet aircraft which were assembled in Chinese aircraft factories. In particular, there are generally thought to be about 2,000 Mig-15, Mig-17 and MiG-19 interceptors and about 300 IL-18 light bombers. It is of some significance for Chinese nuclear potential that the country is still thought to have a handful of old Tu-4 bombers, which was the Russian version of the B-29 heavy bomber of the Second World War. The surface fleet is very modest; but the Soviets made thirty submarines available to the Chinese and these are regarded by the United States as a formidable long-term danger. The central military fact about China, however, is its army of 2,250,000 men. This is the largest army in the world and showed itself in Korea to be both able and adaptable. The quality of the force is now less certain—probably even to its commanders—because it has not seen major action for fifteen years. It has also been used to some extent for economic purposes. Nevertheless, no outsider has dared to commit himself to the suggestion that it might no longer be at its Korean standard; and in the brief campaign against India in 1962 it showed itself to be well-trained and well-commanded.

To this very large and formidable army, the Chinese have now added an ambitious nuclear weapons programme. This has been notable for the fact that it has taken a different direction from the original British and French atomic weapons programmes. Both these countries started with atomic bombs made from plutonium and only very much later built the expensive gaseous diffusion facilities which were needed for hydrogen bombs. China, by contrast, has begun with gaseous diffusion and appears to be directing her efforts towards thermo-nuclear weapons at an early date.

Nothing has yet been published about what aircraft or missiles will carry these weapons. But it is now generally accepted that the Chinese rocket programme, for which test facilities have been observed, is being given a high priority. Great concern has been expressed in the United States at the fact that a Chinese-born rocket technologist with a prominent position in the American programme has returned to China and has apparently taken charge of Chinese missile development. It is to be expected that the earliest rocket developments will be of relatively short range and that these will be followed by longer range weapons, leading ultimately to rockets able to strike at the United States and Europe. Mr McNamara has said that the United States must be prepared for this development by 1975 and expect it by 1980. These dates are not many years away.

With these forces, China looks out on many problems across her frontiers. Almost all of them have led to wars and conflicts in one way or another. Where some powers worry about two fronts, China might be thought to have six simultaneous problems in the great areas which surround her. She has the Soviet Union to the North with the finest army in the world—which with 2,000,000 men is almost as large as the Chinese Army. Beyond the buffer of North Korea, China can see South Korea, where the Americans are well-established and through which the Japanese established themselves on the Asian mainland.

Japan, now an American ally, has the most powerful economy in Asia. Further south, the Nationalist Chinese government is established on Formosa and on the off-shore islands of Quemoy and Matsu. American power has been drawn on to the Asian mainland in Vietnam in very large quantities; and to the west there are long frontiers with India, a rival, and Pakistan, a friend. Seen from Peking, this must represent a vast range of military problems.

Like the Russians before and during the Second World War, Chinese policy has been an enigma to the Western powers—and also to her Asian neighbours. No-one has ever been quite sure about the Peking Government's reasons for particular actions. On one conflict, however, the Chinese Communists have been consistent and clear. This has been their anxiety to complete the conquest of Nationalist China by capturing the offshore islands of Quemoy and Matsu and the large and important island of Formosa, or Taiwan. There have been a number of cases in history of areas remaining independent and having a different history because naval power had become decisive over land power. Formosa comes into this category. The Chinese People's Liberation Army, as it calls itself, could not cross the China Sea; and when it has shown signs that it might be considering a move of this kind the American Seventh Fleet has been interposed. American naval dominance has made a landing on any of these islands—and especially on Formosa—a physical impossibility.

China's entry into the Korean War was more complex. This major conflict between a number of powers—mainly South Korea and the United States—under the banner of the United Nations was not primarily a Chinese affair. The North Korean government was under Russian influence when it launched its aggression against the south in 1950. It was only when the Chinese began to fear that they might lose the buffer state of North Korea between them and the Americans that they decided that they must intervene and attempt to clear the peninsula.

In long and heavy fighting they failed in this objective; but they succeeded in re-creating a substantial North Korea along the armistice line on the 38th parallel. Here they agreed to peace in 1953 and, generally speaking, they have respected this since.

No other border has caused trouble for China on this scale. She has left the colonial enclaves of Hongkong and Macao to their British and Portuguese rulers, at least for the moment. Tibet was occupied by Communist troops in 1951, but revolted in 1959 and this was suppressed with very large forces—probably about 100,000.

With India, the story has been one of bitter disillusionment for the Indians. Under the slogan 'Hindi-Chini Bai Bai', Indian opinion believed strongly that the two most populous nations of the world had evolved five principles of coexistence which contrasted sharply with the warlike habits of others. Indian policy looked to something like a special relationship with China. The Chinese Government responded, however, by questioning the frontiers which India had traditionally claimed and finally launched a major attack on Indian forces in 1962 which resulted in a disaster for Indian arms. Experts on Chinese policy were generally agreed that this was merely intended to establish the historic Chinese frontiers and not to occupy any part of what the Chinese recognized to be India. The war ended when the Chinese fell back of their own accord. Since that time, India has persistently pressed her claim to territory occupied by Chinese forces; but there has been no direct military action.

With Pakistan, by contrast, China has sought and achieved good relations. She has consistently supported the Pakistani case against India and has made a border settlement which the Pakistanis consider to be generous.

This leaves the Soviet Union. As in earlier days with India, Chinese maps show a substantial area of what is now the Soviet Union as Chinese territory. They have not, however, sought to occupy this territory by force of arms.

It remains merely as a claim and presumably as a potent source of bad relations between the two great Communist powers.

Although attempts at reconciliation are made from time to time, most careful observers of Sino-Soviet relations consider that they have become steadily worse over the years. An open and more or less permanent split has been forecast for some time. It is unlikely, however, that this will lead to any form of military tension in the foreseeable future. China is too weak to challenge the Soviet Army, as it did the Indian Army. The Soviet Union is also, of course, a formidable nuclear power. No sane Chinese Government is likely to look for a military conflict in that direction.

This leaves the soft and vulnerable states of south-east Asia, and especially Vietnam. Chinese support for the people of Indochina goes back to the period of revolt against French rule and was given official standing in the Geneva agreements of 1954 which established an international truce supervisory system for Vietnam, Laos and Cambodia. Although this was based on the principle of neutrality, it was widely believed that both Vietnams would be unified under a Communist government. This was resisted by the South Vietnam government which was strongly supported by the United States. Since that time, the Vietcong challenge to the South Vietnam government has grown steadily, with support from both North Vietnam and Peking.

The United States has committed increasing numbers of troops on the other side : and units have also come from South Korea, Australia and New Zealand.

The Vietnam war illustrates well the central thesis of Mao Tse-tung, whose military doctrines laid the foundation for the conquests of the People's Liberation Army. He believes that the countryside should first be taken and then be used to surround and overcome the cities, which are the strongholds of the anti-Communist forces. He sees this both as a doctrine for conquering a country and as a general truth applying to the whole world. In the larger context, the poor countries of the world constitute the countryside and the small number of rich industrial nations the cities. They too, in Mao's eyes, must be surrounded and gradually reduced.

In Vietnam, the effect of the long struggle against the Vietcong has been to draw American power on to the Asian mainland in substantial amounts. Chinese theorists have argued that this is weakening the American position all over the world, including in their own country where the Chinese believe the American Army plays a large part in internal security. There must be concern in Peking at the growth of so great a power in what had been a weak area incapable of offering any challenge to China itself; but any power must be proud to see a small subversive movement in a friendly country tie up so large a part of the power of its main rival.

What kind of power China will be and what she will feel she can safely do with that power remains to be seen. In spite of bold statements about China's ability to survive a nuclear war, there is no evidence that the Chinese leadership is anything but cautious. Its entry into Korea was reluctant : and its two really vigorous acts of aggression—those against India and Tibet—were carefully calculated to achieve specific and realistic objectives within a very short time.

No country can be sure about the success which it will have with industrial development and a country such as China least of all. It is very difficult for it to predict what contact it will have with the outside world and the extent to which it will be able to trade with Japan, the Soviet Union and the Western European countries. There must also be some considerable doubt in Peking about the future of the Communist world and especially of its relations with the Soviet Union. Some hope of special intimacy must remain and especially of Soviet support if the Americans challenge China with nuclear weapons.

Amid these uncertainties, one thing is probably certain : the central object of Chinese policy is to get the Americans out of Asia. At present, the US remains heavily involved both in Vietnam and Korea. The great Chinese hope must be that the experience of Vietnam will be so unproductive and so expensive to the United States that it will once more decide that it cannot afford to become involved on the mainland of Asia. Such a decision consistently applied would achieve the Chinese aim of hegemony throughout southern Asia.

CHAPTER IX

THE EXTENT OF CONFLICT

The great power concentrations of the world are in North America, Europe and China. But most countries are outside these areas and so are most conflicts. This third world is centred on four great continental or semi-continental areas : Latin America, Africa, the Middle East, and the Indian sub-continent. In each of them, the levels of power are much lower than in North America, Europe or China; and there are no powers which now possess nuclear weapons. Yet troops have been used far more frequently in these continents in recent years than in the areas of prime concern to the heavily armed major powers. There have been significant military actions in south-east Asia (Malaya, Vietnam, Borneo), in the Indian sub-continent (the Kashmir War), the Middle East (Egypt-Israel, Suez, the Yemen, the Lebanon, Kuwait, Jordan, Cyprus), Africa (the Congo, Gabon, Kenya, Tanganyika) and Latin America (Guatemala, Cuba, Dominican Republic).

These conflicts have usually had little or nothing to do with the disputes between the Communists and the West which preoccupy the major powers. Perhaps only two since Korea have reflected the Communist/anti-Communist struggle with any clarity. These were the Cuban missile crisis of 1962—a so far unique affair in that it was a direct Soviet-American clash—and the Vietnam struggle.

The origins of most conflicts have to be sought elsewhere. One of the most common causes is the attempt by states to challenge the right of others to exist. The formation of

Malaysia, for example, moved Indonesia to vow to crush it. This led in its turn to a massive effort involving 50,000 British forces who with the Malaysians, Australians and New Zealanders have held the long Borneo jungle border. This has been an expensive campaign, but Malaysia has not been crushed.

The Arab states, particularly Egypt and Iraq, have sought to destroy Israel and have maintained a constant state of war since the foundation of the State of Israel in 1948. The main military activity has been constant Arab raids over the long Israeli borders and occasional retaliatory operations from Israel. Israel and Egypt have been at war with one another since 1948 and have spent heavily to maintain a high standard of military equipment and efficiency.

The long and chaotic Congo operations involving the Katanga Government, the Central Congolese Government and United Nations forces were primarily about a similar but constitutionally different issue : the demand of Katanga for independence, which the central government was resisting. The British reinforcement of Kuwait in' 1961 was provoked because of evidence that Iraq might take military action against the Sheikhdom whose right to exist as a separate state it had always questioned.

India's war with Pakistan in 1965 was about a particular piece of territory : Kashmir. It came after the conflicts over the Rann of Kutch where there are also differences about the border between the two countries. Although Kashmir has been a major source of conflict for many years, the two sides are still on approximately the armistice lines established in the first post-colonial fighting in the 1940s.

The Cyprus troubles of 1965 were about the rights of the Turkish minority in Cyprus which the Turkish Government was prepared to intervene to defend. Here the issues were more subtle and constitutional : but they resolved themselves in the end into disputes about territory within a single country. Many other countries—including Iraq, Egypt, Nigeria, Ghana, and a number of Latin American republics—have had revolutions in which armies played the decisive part.

The military power in these areas is not only very different from the forces in Europe or China but it also varies from one area to another. For example, the United Arab Republic with a population of 29 million has about the same number of tanks as all the twenty republics of Latin America with a population of more than 200 million. They are also very much better and more advanced tanks. Forces in Africa south of the Sahara are considerably smaller and more primitive than those in Latin America. Two examples of specific countries might help to show the pattern.

A typical though larger than average Latin American power is Argentina. Its population of 22,500,000 may be compared to that of Canada; and the total armed forces of 150,000 are not very different in size from the Canadian total of 120,000. But in Argentina, the Army has a strength of 80,000 compared to the Canadian total of 49,000. The Canadian Army serves in Germany, Cyprus and elsewhere and is trained for operations in a major European war or in United Nations peacekeeping. It has no defined domestic role. In Argentina, on the other hand, the Army considers that its primary role is anti-subversion inside the country and the defence of the frontiers.

Both Canada and Argentina maintain one aircraft carrier but the Argentine Navy also has three cruisers. Its concentration on capital ships is unusual for a modern navy. In small escorts, destroyers and frigates, the Canadians have forty while the Argentinians have only ten. Most Latin American ships were acquired from the surpluses of Second World War equipment which such countries as Britain and the United States sold off during their period of run-down after 1945.

The contrast between Argentina and Canada is perhaps

most striking in airpower. The manpower of the Royal Canadian Air Force is almost double that of the Fuera Aerea Argentina and its aircraft are of later design. The five FAA air brigades are operating old types like the Meteor, the Lincoln and the Lancaster which have vanished from the reserves of most other air forces. A large part of this equipment is British in origin. There is, however, a national aircraft factory which assembles the American Mentor trainer and the Paris light jet tactical combat aircraft.

In Africa, Nigeria is scarcely typical in size but her armed forces have the same general character as those of African countries. They remain very small in keeping with the British tradition; and in spite of Nigeria's population of over 50,000,000 the Army has a total strength of only 9,000 men, the Navy 1,500 and the Air Force 1,000. In Europe the Luxembourg Army has 5,500 men, though the Grand Duchy's population is only 1/150 that of Nigeria. In Asia, Indonesia has about double the population of Nigeria but its regular army is about twenty times the size of the Nigerian Army.

For a time after independence, British officers continued to serve in the highest ranks of the Nigerian armed forces. This practice has now been dropped, though there remains a training mission. Most African armed forces have felt that non-alignment can only be served by buying equipment from a variety of different sources; and this is creating severe problems of supply and maintenance. If they have to use their sophisticated arms in battle, they will no doubt also find that they do not have a unified tactical doctrine appropriate to their weapons.

A number of advanced countries have become involved in the training of African air forces. The West Germans have undertaken this role and so have the Canadians. The Nigerians have sent more than 500 pilots and ground personnel to West Germany for training and have bought their aircraft from Germany. They also had a German colonel as commander-in-chief of the Air Force for a time; but, as

F

with the British officers in the Army, this practice has now been dropped.

This sort of equipment and training is difficult to find on a gift basis and the Nigerians have had to pay virtually all their air force costs. The Navy has been more fortunate. It has developed links with the Royal Netherlands Navy and has not only acquired a frigate from Holland but has been given a submarine chaser. The rest of the fleet consists of two minesweeping motor launches, three coastal patrol vessels, two seaward defence vessels and one tank landing craft. By the standards of almost all parts of the world outside Africa, this amount of force must be regarded as negligible. Even inside Africa, there could have been no question of a military operation being mounted against Rhodesia—still less, South Africa—by the countries of the Organization for African Unity. Nevertheless, the control of any country is ultimately in the hands of those who control the most force. The armies of both Nigeria and Ghana showed in the course of 1966 that they were prepared to act politically and could assert their control over the country. In a short space, they murdered Sir Abubakar Balewa in Nigeria and destroyed the regime of Dr Kwame Nkrumah in Ghana. Internally, small armies are just as decisive as large armies.

For all countries outside the main power blocs, the quality of the equipment of the armed forces depends on what they are given and what they are allowed to buy from the main industrial powers. For a wide range of highly-sophisticated equipment, only the United States, the Soviet Union, Britain and France are able to supply what is needed. But for much of the equipment which countries might want, Germany, Canada, Japan, Italy and Czechoslovakia now have a fair range of possibilities : and Sweden and India have some of the important armaments industries.

In the early post-war years, Britain had the predominant share of these markets, including such areas as Latin

America. The Americans concentrated in their sales on western Europe and the Far East. Many armies, navies and air forces still reflect this period in which the weapons which had been decisive in the Second World War were the prestige weapons of the day. Since then, the levels of arms supplies have been raised most where there have been disputes and conflicts. Latin America and Africa have remained at a low level in their equipment; but the Arab countries of the Middle East and Israel have constructed steadily larger and more effective forces in what can only be described as an arms competition. The same has been true on a relatively less ambitious scale in India and Pakistan. The United States, Britain and France tried in the 1950s to regulate the arms flow to Israel and the Arab countries through the Tripartite Declaration, which sought to maintain a balance. This was broken up by the entry of the Soviet Union into the area in committed support of the Arab cause against Israel. France responded by expanding her support of Israel; and important weapons like tanks and submarines have also been supplied to Israel from Britain and anti-aircraft missiles from the United States.

In the Indian sub-continent, the United States decided to make large arms supplies available to Pakistan when it showed itself prepared to join in the Western alliance structure in the containment of the Soviet Union. The Pakistani armed forces have come therefore to be based almost entirely on American equipment. This gave them the advantage of a single system of training and supply to compensate for their numerical inferiority in comparison with India. The Indian policy was to concentrate on developing a large self-sufficient base at home and to buy from various sources of supply. For a long time, their links were mainly with Britain, but increasingly they have turned to the United States (which has been anxious to increase the capacity of the Indian armed forces since the breakdown of Indian-Chnese relations) and to the Soviet Union.

It is thought that the sales of arms in the world outside the great power blocs have now reached something like $1,200,000,000. Of this the Americans and Soviets have perhaps a third each and Britain and France most of the rest. Only about a quarter of the American sales, however, are paid for by the recipients : the rest are covered by grant aid.

Wherever there is conflict, these arms supplies inevitably become a major issue. The United States and Britain incurred deep resentment in India and Pakistan through their decision to stop the supply of arms and spares during the 1965 Kashmir War. This demonstrated the advantages of self-sufficiency to those who might find themselves in prolonged conflicts without the full support of their suppliers.

CHAPTER X

INTERVENTION

There are obviously many reasons why two states resort to force against each other. A dispute between them can be about some small issue which has come to symbolize their pride and dignity; or it can be about really great and fundamental issues, like the rights of Jews and Arabs in what is now Israel. But whether these disputes are resolved by force depends on what national leaders believe can be accomplished by a resort to force. Where the conflict is between great powers, this is mainly a question about what they can do to their rival and what their rival can do to them. Major powers need look only at the direct military consequences which are likely to flow from a clash. Lesser powers have a different range of problems : What effect will their conflict have on the great powers? Will they be able to get supplies and spare parts for military equipment which they have bought abroad? Are others likely to intervene? Will exports, trade and aid be damaged? A resort to force becomes complicated by a wide variety of links with the major powers and with the rest of the world. If it is on anything but the guerilla level of a Vietnam or Yemen, it also has the tendency to raise the temperature in the world. This may force much greater powers to act to stop the conflict if they possibly can.

It can be seen from the great power interventions in recent years that different powers have different ideas of where their interests lie. The most active powers have been the United States and Britain, whose forces have been in-

volved in many situations. The Americans have been involved, particularly, in Latin America, Asia and the Middle
East. The British have been heavily committed to Africa,
the Persian Gulf area and southeast Asia. By contrast, the
Russians and Chinese have confined themselves to their
border areas. These interventions by different governments
are best looked at by continents or areas.

I. *Latin America.* The great areas of the western hemisphere have been a constant preoccupation of the United
States Government. Although the main American forces
are committed to Europe and much larger forces are in
Asia, Latin America can generate an unequalled sense of
urgency in Washington. With the developing belief that
Communist penetration, both Russian and Chinese, was
becoming important, all revolutionary movements have
been seen as a possible threat to the security of the Hemisphere. This process has been encouraged by the Cuban
association with the Soviet Union, which is the first align-
ment of a Latin American republic in modern times with
a major power in the Eastern Hemisphere. An important
part of American policy is now directed towards stopping
the spread of what they regard as the Cuban infection to
other countries.

The United States has been involved in the Caribbean
area since an early stage in her history. In Puerto Rico, the
Canal Zone, and elsewhere, she has direct responsibilities;
and there is a long tradition of direct American military
intervention in the area. Perhaps the most important of
recent years, apart from the Cuban missile crisis, were the
support of the Guatemalan insurgency in 1960, the support of the unsuccessful Cuban landings in 1961, and the
intervention in the Dominican Republic in 1965. Each of
these had something of the same characteristics. They were
all interventions in national conflicts in which one side appeared to the United States to be very much more
desirable than the other; and none of them lasted for any

substantial period of time. Only the Guatemalan intervention was a decisive success. The Bay of Pigs intervention (which did not involve American fighting men) failed very quickly. In the Dominican Republic, American Marines quickly achieved a locally dominant position, but the political issues remained confused.

The Organization of American States has substantial responsibilities for peace and security in the territories of its members. An OAS resolution formed the legal basis for the threatened use of force in the Cuban missile crisis; and the American view is that the organization had a right to intervene in the affairs of its members if there is a threat of Communist rule in the Hemisphere. Not surprisingly, a number of Latin American states resent a system in which they cease to have the sovereign right, theoretically open to all states, to choose the form of government they will enjoy and to make what alignments they choose. To great powers, on the other hand, this notion of a sphere of influence is natural. It is certainly Soviet policy in the Warsaw Pact area—though here it is strongly disputed by the United States—and it is the objective which the Chinese Government is thought to have throughout Southern Asia. A Western European great power might have similar ideas about the Middle East or even Africa.

II. *Asia.* Intervention in Latin America has been important to the United States but the levels of power have been low and the duration of conflict has been short. Asia is a very different matter. It has been the scene of the great conflicts of recent times; and virtually all of these have drawn in some major power at an early stage. The conflicts have been of three types: Communist aggression; guerilla wars led by Communists; and local disputes in which the Communist/non-Communist rivalry played little or no part.

1. *Communist aggression.* There have been four basic situations which had this character, all of them involving

China. All were in the area in which the Chinese Government considers that it should have friendly governments; but each has produced a different response by the other powers. The first was the massive invasion of South Korea by North Korea which was not, in the first instance, a Chinese-provoked war. The Communist North Korean Government was at that time closely linked to the Soviet Government. Their challenge was overwhelming and without subtlety and it demanded either surrender or an equal response. Led by the Americans and blessed by the United Nations Security Council (from which the Soviets at the time were absent), the Western world gave strong and growing support to South Korea. The intervention in support of a country being invaded from the outside was on an unprecedented scale. No doubt this was due in part to the obvious analogy between the *blitzkrieg* type of invasion which the North Koreans employed and the recent experience of the Western powers. The intervention forces suffered heavy losses in two years of tough fighting; but they finally achieved their objective of restoring the integrity of South Korean territory.

In Formosa, intervention has taken a different form. Here the military problem was very much simpler : the United States unilaterally denied the use of the China Sea to Communist Chinese forces. This has involved a deployment of force but no direct conflict.

In Tibet, there has been no attempt at intervention, in spite of the Western claim that the Chinese acted illegally in occupying the province and crushing the later revolt of the people.

In India, in 1962, there was strong Anglo-American interest but no direct intervention. It is possible that the Western powers would have felt compelled to intervene if the Chinese campaign had gone farther and begun to achieve success. When the Chinese forces broke off and conducted a limited withdrawal, the American and British Governments agreed to sponser a large-scale rearmament

programme for the Indian armed forces. This gathered
momentum between 1963 and 1965 when the Indo-
Pakistani war threw it into doubt.

2. *Guerilla Conflicts.* Since the Communist conquest of
China, two countries in Asia have been the scene of large-
scale Communist insurgencies reaching a phase of guerilla
warfare. These are Malaya and Vietnam. Both followed
much the same progression, though the circumstances were
different. In Malaya, the Communists were members of the
Chinese minority in the population and were opposed by
the Malay majority. The Government also had the major
advantage that the peninsula was, in effect, an island cut
off from outside supplies of arms and men. In Vietnam,
the population is effectively homogeneous (with advantages and disadvantages to both sides in comparison with
Malaya) and the insurgents have had relatively easy
access to friendly Communist territory.

In these differing circumstances, the insurgencies have
taken their course. They both began with a period of build-
up of the Communist organization in the villages, gradually
leading to a campaign to destroy the authority of the
government in the countryside. This took the form, primarily, of breaking down communications by destroying
roads and killing government servants who failed to co-
operate. Once control over a large number of villages was
secured, the wars went into their guerilla phase.

Dealing with a challenge of this kind absorbs large numbers of troops. In both Vietnam and Malaya, the original
Western intervention was inevitable, since the insurgencies
were started against European colonial governments. The
French were, after all, directly responsible for the security
of Vietnam and the British for Malaya. Both were drawn
into long and difficult counter-insurgency operations. In
Malaya, this led to the destruction and disintegration of
the Communist forces; in Vietnam, the defeat of the
French at Dien Bien Phu was followed by the Geneva

agreements of 1954 under which many assumed that the whole country would come under Communist rule. The South Vietnam government, supported by the United States, rejected this solution and the United States became increasingly committed to the defeat of the Vietcong guerillas. A second massive anti-guerilla operation was mounted in the 1960s along the same lines as the original operation in the 1950s. This time, however, the Americans tried a new range of techniques. They made an effort to use their massive airpower as a means of compelling North Vietnam to come to favourable terms. On the assumption that the control of the Vietcong was fundamentally in North Vietnam hands, the Americans hoped that by doing serious damage in the North they might reduce the capacity and the will of the Vietcong to fight. Those who had been responsible for the Malayan campaign were sceptical of this. They argued that the Vietcong was not dependent on the North for its supplies, though there was a valuable flow of arms and aid, and that the only way to defeat the insurgency would be to cut the Vietcong off from their supplies of food and men. This meant clearing whole areas of them and giving the villages a reliable defence. There was little success in this direction in the Vietnam campaign under either the French or the Americans.

3. *Conflict outside the East-West dispute.* Although there was a certain element of anti-colonialism in Indonesia's hostility to Malaysia, it certainly involved no challenge by a Communist to a non-Communist power. Indonesia, with a population of 100 million, resented the formation of a Malaysia from Malaya, Singapore and North Borneo. It believed that it was the leader of the Malay people and that an independent state with strong British sponsorship and major British military bases was intolerable. The Indonesian promise to crush Malaysia took the form of a major confrontation along the 900-mile jungle border in Borneo which gradually drew large British, Australian and

New Zealand forces into the area. There were also occasional Indonesian attacks on the Malayan mainland. The Indonesian forces did not, however, attempt a concerted attack across the frontier designed to take and hold territory. The confrontation has remained a confrontation and has not become a war. Nor has any land changed hands as a result of it. The British objective has been to keep it at the lowest possible level; and plans which would disrupt the already weak internal character of Indonesia have been consistently rejected.

The element of outside intervention on the side of Malaysia has been substantial and was until 1965 considerably larger than the American intervention in Vietnam. It arose, however, in certain very special circumstances :

1.   Britain had made a massive and lengthy effort to achieve an independent and non-Communist Malaya.

2.   The settlement which Indonesia challenged, especially in Borneo, had been the object of British government policy.

3.   Britain, Australia and New Zealand had a force permanently stationed in Malaya and Britain had a large naval and air base in Singapore.

A country which was challenged by a neighbour and appealed to the United Nations or to the major powers would not normally enjoy these special circumstances. Nevertheless, it is likely that a threat of totally unjustified military action, such as has been proposed by Indonesia, would force the United States or Britain to support their friends. The readiness to give support of the kind which Commonwealth countries have given to Malaysia can only be seen from each case as it arises. It will obviously depend on particular circumstances. American readiness to give support is obviously influenced by whether the challenge comes from Communists (as in Korea); Britain's willingness has been influenced by whether or not a country is a Commonwealth country. Both of these could be altered by changing alignments.

The war in the Indian sub-continent between India and Pakistan in September, 1965, was marked by the deliberate non-alignment of the major powers. The United States, the Soviet Union, Britain and France were anxious to show that they had no preferences. Only China was an exception to this : she gave her support to Pakistan. Non-intervention took the particularly damaging form—on the part of both the Americans and the British—of a stoppage of deliveries of arms and spare parts to both sides. It probably played a part in bringing the struggle to a rapid conclusion.

None of these Asian situations has been influenced by the South-East Asian Treaty, in spite of the fact that Pakistan is a party to it. The United States Government had hoped in the 1950s that this would be a structure on which a containment of China might be built. When, however, India, Burma and Malaysia declined to join it, its purpose became limited in practice to the defence of Thailand.

III. *The Middle East.* Another organization set up in the same period under British sponsorship, the Central Treaty Organization, was intended to ensure the security of the Middle East against Soviet aggression. Of the Arab countries, only Iraq joined originally : and it withdrew after the revolution of 1958, leaving Britain, Turkey, Iran and Pakistan as the four members. The United States has also played a prominent part. Cento, however, has had little function. There are few contacts between Turkey, Iran and Pakistan. Turkey is in any case in NATO; and Pakistan is not only in SEATO but committed to friendship with China. Just as SEATO has gradually become concentrated on the security problems of Thailand, Cento has been mainly concerned with Iran. An overt Soviet challenge to the South, which seems unlikely, would undoubtedly bring its machinery in to play.

A much more important element of foreign intervention

in this area has been the British forces in the Persian Gulf, with a major base at Aden and air and naval forces on Bahrein. Britain has treaties of guarantee with a large number of Sheikhdoms in the Gulf, the most important of which is Kuwait, an area of immense oil reserves whose right to exist is challenged by Iraq. It was believed in 1961 that Iraq was planning to move on Kuwait. A substantial British force was landed within a few hours but the promised invasion did not materialize.

Britain has decided to leave her base in Aden in 1968 when the South Arabian Federation becomes independent. It is British policy at present to retain a substantial force in the Gulf. If island bases are developed in the Indian Ocean, these would no doubt be used to provide some back up for the amphibious warfare squadron and other forces based on Bahrein. Nevertheless, there will be a decline in the number of formations which will be kept in the area; and there is no sign at present of any other power deploying force in or around the Middle East.

Major Anglo-American interventions in support of existing governments took place almost simultaneously in 1958 in the Lebanon and Jordan. It was believed that both countries were threatened by subversive forces. American troops for the Lebanon, both Army and Marines, were provided from Germany and from the Sixth Fleet in the Mediterranean. The build-up was large-scale and rapid. British forces went into Jordan in much smaller numbers but with the same effect. All these forces were withdrawn within a short time.

There is no reason to believe that an intervention of this kind would not happen again in relatively weak countries threatened by a military plot or some other form of revolution. It is interesting to note, however, that no one seriously considered an intervention by allied forces when the French Government of President de Gaulle faced a revolt of its military forces in Algeria in 1960. Although the President's authority was dependent on a very small number of reliable troops, the position and prestige of France made a use of foreign troops for this purpose inconceivable. Presumably this attitude will take root in many countries which are now prepared to bring in great power friends in a crisis. On the other hand, many of the 130 or more governments in the world rest on a very weak political and military base; and this will probably be true for many years.

A different situation and a different kind of intervention developed in Cyprus in 1964. Here there was no threat to the constituted government; but the open civil warfare which had broken out by the majority Greek community on the minority Turkish community was threatening to bring about a Turkish invasion of Cyprus. The communal slaughter itself was also an affront to the world order. Here once more Britain happened to have troops and these rapidly took control of the situation. The United Nations then undertook to sponsor a peacekeeping force which absorbed the British forces and added substantially to them.

The most important example of an intervention by a new power—indeed by anyone besides the United States, Britain and France—was the Egyptian intervention in the Yemen, where revolutionary forces were trying to establish their regime against Royalist resistance in the hills. This long and expensive campaign put 10,000 Egyptian forces into the same position as the Americans in Vietnam—they controlled the towns but were unable to hold the countryside.

IV. *Africa*. Interventions by the British and French have also been fairly familiar in Africa. Both the Tanganyika and Kenya regimes were saved from Army revolts by rapid British interventions : though there was no question of a similar action by the British in either Nigeria or Ghana. The French acted similarly in Gabon. The breakdown of the Congo led to a large scale intervention by the forces of minor powers under the command of the United Nations.

It is by no means clear what use will be made of force

in Africa in the coming years. The modest use of small amounts of British and French power has been decisive; and there can be little doubt that (apart from South Africa and the Maghreb) those who use even small amounts of force effectively will play a major part in the future of the African Continent.

In the widespread conflicts of the world outside North America and Europe, it is obvious that great power intervention plays an important part. All governments have nominally committed themselves to mutual support against aggression in the Charter of the United Nations—and the pacts and alliances which have been negotiated in considerable numbers since 1949 are based on promises of armed aid if necessary. The United States and Britain (and occasionally France, Australia, Egypt and others) have given this directly. But another form of intervention and support has developed in the name of the United Nations with different rules and more limited freedom of action. The future importance of this kind of intervention is an important and unresolved issue.

CHAPTER XI

UNITED NATIONS PEACEKEEPING

Most of the world belongs to the United Nations, though there are important exceptions like China, the two Germanies, the two Koreas, the two Vietnams and Switzerland. The Charter of the United Nations is an ambitious document which gives the Security Council the right to define a threat to the peace and to do what it considers necessary to deal with it. The Organization even claims the right to override the domestic independence of its members if it identifies such a threat to the peace.

In fact, the United Nations Security Council has almost completely failed to exercise the powers which were so liberally conferred on it at its origins in 1945. The vast grants of power in Chapter VII have gone largely unused. Those who wrote the Charter were determined that when the Allies had achieved their victory over the Fascist powers they would act together to see that these powers did not re-emerge. This time there would be no failure to act until it was too late. But the enemies that were so utterly defeated in 1945 have not re-emerged; and the unanimity which a common enemy gave to the coalition of the Russians, Americans, British and others quickly vanished. The central problem has been to maintain peace among the victorious allies : and since the Security Council could not act against the will of any one of its permanent members—the United States, the Soviet Union, Britain, France or China—it has taken no direct part in the confrontations of the major powers. Chapter VII of the Charter has been all but a dead letter.

Nevertheless, the United Nations has been an important intervention power. In ways which no-one had predicted, it found itself drawn into one situation after another. While the Military Staffs Committee of the Security Council has remained an entirely useless body, troops in the blue helmets of the United Nations have been serving at a large proportion of the difficult situations all around the world.

In the early days of the UN, it sent troops or observers to the troubled situations in Greece, Indonesia, Kashmir and Palestine. Experience was gathered and it was generally felt that the world concern with dangerous situations made the United Nations a valuable instrument for these purposes. In the much vaster conflagration in Korea, the United Nations Security Council initiated an enforcement action under Chapter VII of the Charter : but this was done when the Soviet Union was boycotting the United Nations and there has always been doubt about whether the Charter applied in these circumstances. At any rate, it seems likely that none of the five permanent members of the Security Council will allow the Council to act in its absence again. They will attend and veto if there is something proposed which they do not approve. So an action of this kind against the line of the Soviets can be regarded as unique and most unlikely to be repeated.

The first major intervention by the general decision of the organization was the United Nations Emergency Force which was sent into Suez in 1956. This whole operation was undoubtedly a striking success. It ended the long period of raiding across the border of the Gaza Strip and effectively ended the Arab-Israeli guerilla struggle : and it provided a cover under which British and French forces were successfully evacuated. Ten years later, UNEF forces are still in the Gaza Strip; there has been little improvement in the political situation and no solution to the basic problems of the area; but the UN has taken violence out of the conflict.

The success of UNEF suggested that the UN was ready for

G

larger things; and when the Congo disintegrated in 1960 a remarkable force was built up from countries which were not members of either the North Atlantic Treaty or the Warsaw Pact. This practice was established because of the deep fear on both sides that the forces of the major powers might be drawn into this distant African country and come into conflict with one another. Indians, Swedes, Irish, Ethiopians, Nigerians and Ghanaians made up the force, though their transport had to be provided by the Americans. Small numbers of committed forces were used for technical tasks but all the fighting arms had to pass the strict test of non-alignment.

These troops, once committed, had to work out just what the object and methods of the United Nations should be. There can be little doubt that more force was used in the Congo than the UN should have used; that many of the troops were not trained for the police work which is the essence of UN action (though some, notably the Nigerians, were); and that the political objectives of the UN in trying to get foreign mercenaries out of the Congo involved them in action which at times was more enforcement than peace-keeping.

There were also enormous problems of finance, of command, of organization and of discipline. The United Nations established certain basic principles about how it should go into an action of this kind. In particular, it insisted on an agreement with the legitimate government guaranteeing freedom of movement for UN troops and the right to use force in self-defence.

The experience of the Congo was deeply depressing to the UN. Congolese politics changed continuously in the course of the operation and it was seldom clear what the United Nations forces should be trying to achieve. United Nations officials fell into primitive and threatening hands and its forces were humiliated for a time by the attacks of two armed jet trainer aircraft to which they had no reply. The Secretary-General of the United Nations handled the complex political issues with the authority of his own office; and in the process found himself up against hostile opposition from the Soviet Union and also France and Britain. Only the United States among the great powers supported the way in which the campaign was conducted from beginning to end.

As a result of the Congo, there was strong pressure for a development of a much higher level of training and efficiency among UN forces. It was realized that the organization could not recruit its own troops and have its own forces. The cost would be far beyond its budget and the demands on a standing force would soon outrun any conceivable capacity. There was also general agreement that the Charter system of great power forces committed to the Security Council is not appropriate to the kind of situation into which the United Nations has been drawn. Its function has been to hold the ring without involving the major powers. Apart from transport and other services, it has therefore found it essential to avoid using the forces of the United States and Soviet Union.

The experience of the Congo therefore led to a request by the Secretary-General to the members of the UN to prepare troops for peacekeeping operations and to provide the necessary organization on a purely national basis. A number of countries have responded including Canada, the Scandinavians, Brazil and the Netherlands. Units have been specially set aside for UN duties and trained in the sort of techniques which experience has suggested will be needed.

The next major peacekeeping operation had none of the chaos of the Congo. This was the outbreak of communal fighting in Cyprus in 1963 in which the Greek majority's treatment of the Turkish minority brought a threat of Turkish intervention. This case was seriously influenced by the fact that Britain had troops on the island and properly equipped sovereign bases under British control. A pacification operation has been undertaken by the British on their own; and in 1964 this was converted into a United Nations operation, with British, Canadians, Finns, Irish and Swedes serving under an Indian commander. Here the Congo troubles have not been repeated. The basic staff services were all present in the British command and this has made the whole operation very simple to keep under clear and efficient control. The UN has learned the advantage of having a substantial power at the centre of the operation; but it has also come up against a more fundamental problem which had suggested itself in earlier operations. This is how to extricate itself from a situation in which it has become a part of the local military stability; and arising from this, how it is to be financed over a substantial period.

The problem in Cyprus is an endemic one : a long-term clash which is only likely to be settled by some solution like partition, which everybody rejects. The effect of the United Nations presence is to take the urgency out of the difficult problem of finding a solution. But to maintain troops on this scale is going to cost someone a great deal of money. For the moment, the British and Canadian troops are being financed by their governments. But the cost of peacekeeping operations are sinking the United Nations deep into debt; and long-continued efforts in places like Cyprus could become an impossible burden. French and Soviet hostility to paying for operations which they do not approve has come close to breaking up the United Nations.

Gradually, however, the UN is getting some idea of what it can and cannot do to sustain the world order. What the UN is, in essence, is the agent of the major powers; and though the Charter has so far been proved wrong in its idea that they would act together to keep the peace the basic notion has proved to be right. For in any outbreak which threatens to draw them in they must operate by the same rules : and the function of the UN has been to find an area of common ground between them. When it has

UNIVERSITY OF VICTORIA
LIBRARY
Victoria, B. C.

used force, the essence of its method has been to employ troops who are not unacceptable to any of the powers concerned. This has been a delicate political operation : and its purpose has been to provide the minimum of order in the situation without arousing the hostile power blocs.

Any list of UN operation shows that there are certain areas of the world in which they have been concentrated. Where there are large local forces or a predominant great power interest, the United Nations has been less active. In Latin America, the United States has preferred to work through the Organization of American States, reporting subsequently on what it has done to the Security Council. The Soviets have taken direct action in the Warsaw Pact area. In Asia, the UN has taken a part only in peripheral situations like the transfer of West Irian from the Netherlands to Indonesia (in which Pakistani ,troops were used).

The main demands on the United Nations have been made from three areas : the Mediterranean, the Middle East and Africa. Each time, it has been obvious that intervention by someone was essential to stop some situation from disintegrating. But the organization has shown very little capacity to use its machinery according to the original design. The necessary unanimity of the great powers has not been there. There is only one clear case of an enforcement action as anticipated by the Charter : the Security Council resolution of April, 1966, empowering Britain to take action to prevent oil tankers from entering the port of Beira with oil destined for Rhodesia. For all other peacekeeping, the UN has had to rely on what corners of the Charter were available to it. In the end this has meant exploiting a combination of the power of the General Assembly to recommend and the natural authority which has been attached to the office of the Secretary-General. This authority was used in the Congo, in particular, by Mr Dag Hammarskjoeld. Under his successor, U Thant, there has been no such vast and unforeseen demand on the peacekeeping capacity of the UN; and it may be doubted whether the organization would feel capable of undertaking something on this scale after the troubles it encountered in planning, commanding and financing the Congo struggle.

There remains the vast power possessed by the Security Council if the United States, the Soviet Union, Britain, France and whatever China holds the seat can agree to act. Both the Soviet Union and France have made it clear that they are not prepared to be drawn into United Nations peacekeeping actions on any basis other than Chapter VII enforcement. It is still possible, however, that for some purposes Chapter VII may come to be used. The growth of a common interest between the Soviets and the West in peace in wide areas of the world has been shown in a number of recent situations and especially in the India-Pakistan conflict of 1965. There has also been unity in the approach to Rhodesia. The great powers, and especially the Soviet Union, may also conclude that by blocking the use of the Security Council they have stimulated the growth of other agencies of power in the United Nations; and that to allow a reasonable level of action by the Security Council itself would keep the old Charter system alive and with it their right to veto. So far, however, only the Beira oil tankers have attracted the unqualified interest of the Security Council : and the peacekeeping emergencies continue to fall into the hands of a Secretary-General who is allowed neither the staffs nor the money to handle them.

CHAPTER XII

DISARMAMENT

No government is prepared to say it is content with the world order as now established. Although the major powers feel that the balance of terror offers a high degree of security, they all feel that there are dangers. New weapons seem certain to come along. The present weapons of mass destruction are moving constantly into new hands and opening a wide range of uncertainties. No-one has any clear idea how order is to be kept among the small nations and what will be done to deal with aggression or chaos if the great powers are not united. However well the will of governments may be tested by their rivals, new men can come along. This renews the possibility of miscalculation, as with the classic Soviet miscalculation of President Kennedy in 1962. The weapons of mass destruction, of world cataclysm, remain : and as long as they remain they can be used. There is undoubted strength and stability in the present system. But it contains serious risks if prolonged indefinitely.

Almost every government officially concedes this. They go on to proclaim the need to abolish most or all armaments. In recent years this tendency has gone much further than ever before with the arrival of systematic plans for general and complete disarmament. The Soviet Union took the lead in promoting this idea in 1959—though it had its roots in traditional Soviet proposals—and most other powers have followed. In the course of 1962, massive plans purporting to rid the world of all arms not needed for internal police purposes were published under the names of the governments of the United States and the Soviet Union. The United Nations and the Commonwealth both gave the idea their formal support.

The Soviet and American proposals have been negotiated in Geneva at the Eighteen-Nation Disarmament Committee since that time.

These negotiations, however, have never become at all serious. Both sides have accused the other of putting forward a plan which would work to their military advantage in the earlier stages. There has been a long and complex dispute over the differing approaches of the Soviets and the West to inspection and control by international authorities. The debate probably reflects a fundamental reluctance to consider far-reaching disarmament; but it has also revealed a basic difference about the kind of disarmed world which each is imagining. Even the most modest arms control measures (like the partial nuclear test ban) come up against this contrasting approach.

The basic difference between the two is to be found in the long-term character of power at the end of the disarmament process. The United States has a picture of a world which gradually becomes dominated by the United Nations. Its United Nations Peace Force, as it calls it, would be the predominant power in the world and would not be subject to a veto over its use by what are now the super-powers. The United States has not made up its mind just what authority would be able to use this decisive force (and this must be the key to their whole plan, since domination of the world is at stake); but they are quite clear about the basic notion that as the power of individual states declines the power of the centre must be built up. American thinkers deny that this would necessarily mean world government. They believe that a single monopoly of power should exist in the service of world law. Very little work has been done on the command, organization, bases, financing and, above all, the right to use the UN Peace Force;

but the general picture in the American mind is clear enough.

The Soviet approach is fundamentally different. They have stuck solidly throughout all disarmament negotiations to the idea that true international forces are out of the question. Even in the fully disarmed stage, they want peace-keeping to be done by forces which are committed to the Security Council by the unanimous decision of the permanent members. They are not prepared to contemplate an international use of force against the will of the permanent members of the Security Council.

There is also a quite fundamental difference between these two powers about how much force there should be in the world. The American-style United Nations Peace Force is obviously a considerable power in its own right. It would have to be able to act decisively in local situations wherever they might develop, which means good transport and substantial and mobile forces. The United States government has never come down clearly on the question of nuclear weapons—whether, that is, they should be abolished altogether or should become a monopoly of the UN Peace Force. But since at present there is no foreseeable way of ensuring that secret stocks of these weapons do not still exist after they have nominally been abolished, most American thinking prefers the retention of a nuclear deterrent in the hands of the United Nations Peace Force.

The Soviets have stuck to their position that there should be a complete abolition of nuclear weapons and that national forces should be reduced to the kinds of militia and police needed to maintain internal law and order. Peacekeeping operations would be made up from these forces. Although at one stage the Soviet Government conceded that there would be no way to find concealed nuclear weapons, it has stuck to its preference for agreement to abolish these weapons completely. .

All this suggests a quite fundamental difference between

H

the two traditional sides to disarmament negotiations. But behind these differences there must be doubt about whether in anything like the present state of the world either the United States or the Soviet Union would agree to carry out their own proposals. In the American case, official spokesmen have always insisted that the three stages of the plan for general and complete disarmament cannot have their time-scale written in : and that the third stage, in particular, must be seen to be very distant. The Soviets, on the other hand, have been very much more bold. They have said that they would like a rapid timetable in which the whole process down to complete disarmament would be achieved in four years. Their seriousness cannot be gauged since they know that the West is unwilling to give up the security of its arms, that it rejects fundamentally the anarchy of disarmed national states without a world force, and that it does not believe that anything like this would be possible in a short space of years. They are sure of rejection and so safe to advocate what they see fit.

These differences might be called strategic. The central objective and the timing are in dispute. But there are also major tactical differences, and these have been the main source of debate in the disarmament negotiations of recent years.

The central tactical dispute has concerned the subject of inspection. On one question after another, the Soviets have argued that the West is seeking inspection without disarmament or that at any rate the West is putting inspection ahead of disarmament—that, in short, many Western disarmament proposals are a crude attempt at spying. The West has objected that it is impossible to agree on what should be disarmed if there is no evidence about what exists. If it is decided that each side ought to reduce to 500 tanks, it is necessary to know how many tanks they have now; and it is necessary to inspect the tanks which remain to see that they do not exceed 500. It is also necessary to verify that no new tank production is going on.

Here there is a difference between the approach of the United States and the Soviet Union to the problems of military secrecy. The combination of an open society and a Congressional system of government have led the United States to abandon the traditions of secrecy for a large part of the basic information about her armed forces. This process has perhaps gone farther in the United States than in any other country : and certainly the contrast with the Soviet Union is striking. Very little military information is published by the Soviet Government. Occasionally some statistics are given for a particular purpose, but even the Soviet delegates to the Geneva Disarmament Committee have had to rely on Western publications for basic facts for use in debates about the security which would remain under various disarmament proposals.

It is hardly surprising, therefore, that there have been persistent Soviet-American debates about inspection. The Soviets have insisted that they cannot permit inspection unless there is disarmament; and that if the Western powers want to have general inspection of the Soviet Union they will have to accept general disarmament. Inspection must not precede disarmament. The West has insisted that inspection must be adequate to make it certain that any agreement is being carried out. If this means inspecting what is not being abolished as well as what is being abolished, there is nothing that can be done about it.

One largely unpublicized technical development may be helping to ease this problem. Agreement to formal inspection has always been unnecessary to the extent that national methods of finding out information were adequate. Put in Soviet terms, if the West can succeed in spying by other means, it will not need to use disarmament agreements as an intelligence technique.

There is at present good grounds for believing that a great deal more information is available to the United States about the Soviet Union because of the development of reconnaissance satellites which continuously photograph large areas of ground beneath them. This is an expensive process, both in the large satellite telescopes which are needed and in the staffs which are required to make anything useful of the information. Nevertheless, it is probable that it is making the United States very much more certain about what the Soviet Union has : or, put another way, it has already installed something of an inspection system without any need for Soviet consent.

While the vast general and complete disarmament plans remain on the table and are occasionally debated, realistic hopes are mainly attached to what are generally referred to as collateral measures. These are partial measures of disarmament of various kinds which it is hoped will make the world safer and which might also help to make the general disarmament process possible.

The best years for these were 1963 and 1964—mainly, no doubt, because the world situation was favourable (and because of the shocks to the whole system of the Cuban missile crisis). Whatever the reason, four agreements of various kinds were reached in this period. The first and most important was the partial ban on nuclear testing, which was negotiated by the United States, the Soviet Union and Britain and has since been signed by 112 other states, ninety-five of which have ratified it. The most significant absentees are France and China, both of which have conducted nuclear tests since the agreement was signed and intend to continue.

The ban covers all nuclear tests in the atmosphere, underwater and outside the atmosphere, but it does not cover underground tests. The three original signatories have conducted a long debate about the problem of inspecting underground tests, which most Western opinion believes would require some right of on-site inspection. This meant giving the inspectors the right to go on to Soviet soil when they had detected activity on their seismographs which had some of the characteristics of a nuclear explosion. The three other forms of nuclear testing are easily monitored from outside the country and so did not raise the troubled problem of inspection on Soviet soil.

During 1964, two more agreements were reached. The study of nuclear crises, especially in the United States, had led to the conclusion that a central difficulty was communication. In a tense situation or an actual outbreak of war, bargaining and negotiation were likely to become more difficult just at the time when they were most important. This led to the idea that a permanent communications link should be created between Moscow and Washington and constantly manned. Popularly known as the 'hot line', this was agreed and set up. It was revealed late in 1965 that it had not yet been used, a reflection less of the wisdom of the idea than of the success of the major powers in avoiding a major crisis.

Although the communications link travels through London, this was a purely bilateral arrangement. It was followed by another purely Soviet-American agreement. The two powers recorded their intention not to place weapons of mass destruction in orbital vehicles. Since no other power was in a position to do this, no other adherents were invited. This agreement could be important as a statement of mutual restraint, but it offended against the usual American requirements by making no provision for inspection. It also left open the possibility of orbital weapons which might be held in readiness for a crisis and be put up as a bargaining weapon or as a terror threat when required.

Finally, the United States and the Soviet Union announced a simultaneous cut-back in the production of fissile material for weapons. Britain had made the same announcement some months earlier but it had not occurred to her that this might be presented as a disarmament initiative. In fact, the lower levels of production were ordered because the three original nuclear powers had large growing stocks and were anxious to reduce these expensive and increasingly useless industries. There was no inspection nor was there a commitment not to increase production again.

Throughout 1965 and 1966, the main subject of negotiation and debate was a proposed non-proliferation agreement for nuclear weapons. This would contain two basic provisions : that the nuclear powers (which would include China) would agree not to give or sell nuclear weapons to the non-nuclear powers : and that the non-nuclear powers would agree not to manufacture or acquire them. Obviously, the most difficult part of this proposal is the second part; and such countries as Sweden, India and Germany have expressed strong reservations. It is difficult to see how the nuclear powers can succeed in inducing all the non-nuclear powers to accept a non-nuclear status permanently while the original five are free to do what they like.

In the Geneva debate, however, the central dispute has been over the obligations of the nuclear powers and not those who are to be formally classified as non-nuclear. The Soviet Union has been insisting on a Western undertaking not to enter into any form of nuclear sharing with Germany and has asked for a wording which ruled out any NATO nuclear force at any time. Britain has also expressed modified criticism of the American wording on the ground that it leaves open some theoretical possibility of a change in control at some future date. Other proposals of recent interest in Geneva have been mainly American in origin : an uninspected cut-off in fissile material production (which might put real teeth into a non-proliferation agreement); the destruction of obsolete bombers; an agreement to produce no new strategic nuclear delivery systems; and an agreement that the moon and planets shall remain free of weapons and open to all.

Taken overall, there can be little doubt that the whole disarmament debate is in a very bad way. Both the Soviet and American general disarmament proposals are far removed from reality. Orthodox American opinion is anxious to stabilize and secure the present arms structure rather than dismantle it; and the same is probably true of those

who are responsible for Soviet security. But there is no obvious solution to the dangers of conflict in third world
situations, of new and ever more terrible weapons, and
above all of the steady emergence of new powers each of
whose arrival threatens to crack the hardening structure
of the balance of terror.

CHAPTER XIII

THE PROSPECTS FOR PEACE

There are deep differences of opinion among thoughtful people about whether a disarmed world would be safer and better than the world we now have. But most informed people would agree that, good or bad, desirable or undesirable, it is unlikely to happen. Unless governments change their outlook very sharply and believe that the security they are now getting from their arms is rapidly dwindling, major disarmament proposals are likely to be rejected. The disarmament dialogue between the Soviet Union and the United States and her allies is at a very low level. Its claim to be a negotiation is ridiculous. In spite of years of effort, very little has been accomplished; and in addition, France does not give her assent to the Western position and the views of China have not yet been sought.

We must therefore calculate that our world will remain heavily armed. The confrontations may change. Old disputes may wither away and with them the arms on both sides which surround them. But with 130 possible disputants of all levels of power (and a number of ideologies) there are many possibilities for new disputes. The central problem of power will be to see that these do not lead by some progression to disaster.

From the emergence of thermo-nuclear weapons in the middle 1950s, the capacity of armed forces to devastate the whole earth has been beyond dispute. Those most closely concerned with the problem have almost all come to the conclusion that this has sharply reduced the likelihood of major war. Many argue that rational war is out of the question and that the only problems are accident and madness. Others see a continuing danger of miscalculation, with a far higher price to be paid for error. Even in the dark periods of challenge and counter-challenge which surrounded the Berlin and Cuban crises, few statesmen or military men seriously believed that there was a strong chance of a world conflagration. With the lessons of these crises now generally known, optimism is even stronger. Those who argued that the balance of terror was the central fact and that all else would in the end submit to it have so far been proved right.

In the West, at any rate, the idea of stability has taken deep root. New weapons and new strategies are judged on the impact they will have on the stability of the Soviet-American relationship. The old fear of an atomic Pearl Harbour in which the missiles would drop without warning from the sky has vanished. The Soviets may be an enigma : but on the issue of major war with the NATO powers there is no longer much doubt about their views. They want to avoid it at all costs. Those in authority in the West find the decision to embark on world war equally inconceivable. Even those on both sides who insist on a strong deterrent posture—an insistence that they really are prepared to use nuclear weapons early and massively—do so because they feel it puts war completely out of the question. We can conclude that there is great stability in the present Soviet-American confrontation. The risks that it will fail are not great, at least in the years which can be foreseen.

But while the risk might be small, the cost of failure is immeasurable. A small chance of a great calamity can be every bit as serious as a strong chance of a lesser misfortune. Stability weights the odds heavily in favour of restraint and peace. But he would be a bold man who said that it was more than extremely favourable odds—that in fact it was a certainty. There are few if any certainties in history.

The uncertainties are unfortunately increased by a number of possibly dangerous developments. Undoubtedly the most serious of these is the fact that there is not a simple Soviet-American confrontation; and that with every year that passes it becomes clearer that new actors are going to make their presence felt on the world stage. Nuclear proliferation is the symbol of this: but it is not nuclear weapons specifically so much as the general emergence of powerful and independent units which complicates the popular picture of a stable and permanent balance.

At present, the central problem is obviously China. Industrially, she now rates as a middle power; and in position, ambition and size she must be expected to play a growing part in the world order. Japan, too, will one day abandon her present exclusive concentration on economic development. She seems certain to convert some of her industrial power into military strength. What form this will take and what her alignments will be no-one can predict—least of all the Japanese themselves. The way forward is not clear; and the strength of the American system is such that it satisfies the Japanese for the present.

This is also true of West Germany, which with Britain and France is searching for the right relationship with the United States and the Soviet Union. All three Western European powers have shown interest in a political union. If this were to come about, the new Europe would certainly be on the same scale as the United States or the Soviet Union in power. How this would affect the stability of the balance or what new alignments would emerge is exceptionally difficult to predict.

There are, of course, many other areas which might eventually come to play a leading part in the structure of world power. For the present, it seems possible to predict that China, Japan, Germany and possibly Western Europe will be seeking a place and will be trying to understand how they might find effective influence in the system. If the world order does absorb them, we will obviously not be left with a simple balance of terror based on two super-powers. A complex balance of terror may be even more terrifying and so even more effective than one with only two sides. But it will introduce new uncertainties. They will have to be handled intelligently and without miscal-culations about what other people are trying to do or how they are likely to respond.

The second difficulty is technological. There is always the possibility that at some stage one or more major powers may get the capacity to destroy the entire nuclear forces of his rival. With the development of the rocket-firing nuclear-powered submarine, this is difficult to foresee; but the whole trend of technology has been towards an increase in the striking power and precision of weapons. Over time, they must be expected to become more destructive and more accurate. Invulnerability could be difficult to sustain. At any rate, some government might come to believe that the combination of a massive surprise attack with an ap-parently effective anti-ballistic missile system was enough to make its country secure. If this day comes, it is still dis-tant. But it remains a threat hidden inside the unknown world of technology.

The third danger is human. Governments change very rapidly and men come into power who do not understand what has gone before. All countries have a tendency to bring men into high office who are experts on other sub-jects, like the domestic economy. Few junior politicians now concern themselves with security problems. The strategic theorists tend to assume that the lessons of Cuba or what-ever it might be have been learned. But while Mr Khrushchev and Mr Kennedy may have gained a profound understanding of how to live with nuclear power, both these men have passed from the scene. There is a limit to how often lessons like this can safely be re-learned.

Finally, and perhaps most important, there is the dan-ger of conflict outside the area of great power confronta-tion. This could come about in many different ways. Perhaps the most obvious and the most dangerous is a Soviet (or ultimately a Chinese) decision to intervene directly in the defence or support of friendly powers outside their present sphere of influence. It has been Soviet policy to avoid commitments of this kind; and, generally speaking, this has been successful except in the case of Cuba. But this policy could be reversed.

In the Cuban case, a government in bitter conflict with the United States declared itself for international Communism and appealed for Soviet support. The result was that the Soviets were drawn into an untenable position and one which might have been very dangerous. Others are bound from time to time to look to Moscow for protection. In spite of the Kremlin's traditional reluctance, there might be no realistic alternative. The pressures of public opinion and the obligations of leadership in the Communist movement might force a Soviet government to unpredictable commitments which could bring it into serious conflict with the West.

If the Soviet Union became a power ready and willing to operate its armed forces around the world (on the Anglo-American pattern), there would be strong pressures to form spheres of influence so as to avoid Soviet-American conflict. But this can impose agonizing choices on those who have to watch their friends being defeated outside their own sphere of influence. The West was deeply distressed by the terrible events in Hungary in 1956; but the need to stay out was reinforced by the conviction that the predominance of the Soviet forces in that area was overwhelming. In other parts of the world, the Western powers will have more possibilities open to them. The one kind of arms race which could become serious in the 1970s would be a development of long-range mobility in the Soviet Union and an attempt by the Americans, British and perhaps others to maintain the great superiority of the Western powers in this category of power.

In sum, then, the prospects for world peace seem very

good; but there are grave dangers to be constantly over-come.

There is undoubtedly a system working and it has real strength. The difficulty is that the system can only be seen for what it is when it is tested. Like a blindfold man who is only occasionally allowed a glimpse of what surrounds him or the illumination of a pinball machine when the ball strikes a wire, we cannot find out what the system is except in the dangerous crisis of choice. Only the North Korean invasion of South Korea showed clearly that in this case (1) the United States and some of her allies were prepared to make heavy sacrifices for the defence of this distant part of Asia and (2) that nuclear weapons would not be used. Neither of these was, of course, inevitable. Different decisions might have been taken by different men. But the forces which were working on President Truman would have placed any other President under similar constraints.

Decision will in the end be in the hands of men. Strong as the system might be, they are subject to all the weaknesses of human beings. They may be vain; they may be given to anger; they may even, from time to time, have ceased to be entirely sane.

We probably face the prospect of a long continued peace in the presence of weapons of mass destruction. New men who have known nothing else may decide that a bold use of power will improve their own and their country's position. Speaking different languages and possessing different ideologies, they could seriously miscalculate the response of others. The consolation must be that in testing the system they will illuminate it once again; and that if control is not lost they will act so as to survive.

It is possible that in all this the hopes of a safer world will gradually increase. As more security decisions are taken by individual governments with an eye to stability and the maintenance of the existing order, this order may find it grows deeper roots. Governments acting singly may discover that they have constructed something new which serves their common interest in security. Dimly understood, this already exists. The struggle for peace is to give it an enduring life, with the flexibility to meet changing political facts, without releasing the forces of destruction.